Translation and Travelling Theory

Research has shown that feminist theory has flowed far more easily from North to South and from West to East, whereas travel in other directions has proved almost non-existent. While the hegemony of US feminist theory has been challenged in Europe, for example, there remain many 'invisible' discursive trajectories that link the development of feminist theories and movements across the world. This book brings together and engages with theories of globalisation, transnational feminism, travelling theory and cultural translation, exploring the travelling routes of feminist theory and practice to China over recent decades. With attention to the crucial questions of why and how knowledge travels or fails to travel, the forms that it takes and by whom it is sent, received, understood, translated, or even refused, the author examines the development and activities of different groups of women and women's organisations in China, thus developing an alternative form of travelling theory. A study of the cross-cultural translation of knowledge and practices that occur or fail to occur when different cultures interact, and their impact, this book will appeal to scholars of gender studies, sociology, and cultural studies with interests in feminist thought and the travel and production of knowledge.

Min Dongchao is Director of the Centre for Gender and Cultural Studies and Professor in the Department of Cultural Studies at Shanghai University, China.

The Feminist Imagination- Europe and Beyond

Series Editors:

Kathy Davis,
Kathy Davis is Senior Research Fellow at the Vrije University, Amsterdam, The Netherlands

Mary Evans,
Mary Evans is Visiting Professor at the Gender Institute at the London School of Economics and Political Science, UK

For a full list of titles in this series, please visit: www.routledge.com

With a specific focus on the notion of 'cultural translation' and 'travelling theory', this series operates on the assumption that ideas are shaped by the contexts in which they emerge, as well as by the ways that they 'travel' across borders and are received and re-articulated in new contexts. In demonstrating the complexity of the differences (and similarities) in feminist thought throughout Europe and between Europe and other parts of the world, the books in this series highlight the ways in which intellectual and political traditions, often read as homogeneous, are more often heterogeneous. It therefore provides a forum for the latest work that engages with the European experience, illuminating the various exchanges (from the USA as well as Europe) that have informed European feminism. The series thus allows for an international discussion about the history and imaginary of Europe from perspectives within and outside Europe, examining not only Europe's colonial legacy, but also the various forms of 'cultural imperialism' that have shaped societies outside Europe. Considering aspects of Europe 'abroad' as well as Europe 'at home', this series is committed to publishing work that reveals the central and continued importance of the genealogy of feminist ideas to feminism and all those interested in questions of gender.

Published titles in this series

Transatlantic Conversations: Feminism as Travelling Theory
Kathy Davis and Mary Evans
(Ashgate, 2011)

Framing Intersectionality: Debates on a Multi-Faceted Concept in Gender Studies
Helma Lutz, Maria Teresa Herrera Vivar and Linda Supik
(Ashgate, 2011)

Translation and Travelling Theory

Feminist theory and praxis in China

Min Dongchao

LONDON AND NEW YORK

First published 2017
by Routledge
2 Park Square, Milton Park, Abingdon, Oxon OX14 4RN

and by Routledge
711 Third Avenue, New York, NY 10017

Routledge is an imprint of the Taylor & Francis Group, an informa business

© 2017 Min Dongchao

The right of Min Dongchao to be identified as the author of this work has been asserted in accordance with sections 77 and 78 of the Copyright, Designs and Patents Act 1988.

All rights reserved. No part of this book may be reprinted or reproduced or utilised in any form or by any electronic, mechanical, or other means, now known or hereafter invented, including photocopying and recording, or in any information storage or retrieval system, without permission in writing from the publishers.

Trademark notice: Product or corporate names may be trademarks or registered trademarks, and are used only for identification and explanation without intent to infringe.

British Library Cataloguing in Publication Data
A catalogue record for this book is available from the British Library

Library of Congress Cataloging-in-Publication Data
A catalog record for this book has been requested

ISBN: 978-1-4724-4872-9 (hbk)
ISBN: 978-1-315-54993-4 (ebk)

Typeset in Bembo
by Apex CoVantage, LLC

To my mother Tian Benna and my father Min Ren

'In this vitally important narrative, Min Dongchao skillfully weaves feminist theory, historical scholarship, and personal experience into her examinations of the power-inflected intricacies of notions of "travel" and "translation" alongside the idiosyncratic pathways of academic and activist openings in post-Mao Chinese feminisms. Highly recommended for anyone interested in understanding the evolution of feminist and intellectual discourses in China today.'

Sharon R. Wesoky, Allegheny College, USA

Contents

	Acknowledgements	viii
1	Introduction: how far does travelling theory travel? Questions for travelling theory and translation	1
2	Awakening again: the 1980s	17
3	*Duihua* (dialogue) in-between: the process of translating the terms 'feminism' and 'gender' in China	40
4	*Jiegui* (connecting with the international track): the 1990s	71
5	The cases of two NGOs	91
6	That was the past, what is the future?	116
	References	128
	Index	139

Acknowledgements

The main theme of the book is travelling theory. On the long journey to accomplishing this book, I have been accompanied by many people along the way.

I give my heartfelt thanks and appreciation to my friends, colleagues and associates in women's studies throughout China. They shared their time, life and passion with me in my fieldwork in China during 1999 and 2003. I write of my interviewees: Du Fangqin, Fang Lian, Fang Qing, Gao Xiaoxian, Ge Youli, Ji Xuemei, Jin Yihong, Li Huiying, Li Xiaojiang, Li Yi, Liu Bohong, Sheng Ying, Sun Xiaomei, Tan Shen, Wen Yiqun, Zhang Kaining, Zhao Jie, Zhao Qun, Zheng Bijun, Zheng Fan, Yang Guocai, and Yang Hong.

My special thanks go to the scholars and activists involved in my two case study groups: the Yunnan Reproductive Health Research Association (YRHRA) and the Chinese Society for Women's Studies (CSWS).

My deep thanks also go to members of our team in the research project "Development Project Design, Analysis and Implementation" from Yunnan Gender and Development (YGAD): Li Chunrui, Tong Jiyu, and Yang Jing.

This book is based on and is an extension of my PhD research project which I started in 1997 in the women's studies programme at the University of Manchester. My thanks go first to the members of the women's studies group, and especially to my supervisor Professor Liz Stanley for her trust, encouragement, and keen critical faculties which were crucial in directing me in defining my PhD project. I owe a great debt of gratitude for the influence of her academic professionalism, which I have often fallen back on during my academic career.

In 2003, I received the Rockefeller Fellowship on "Gender and Globalization in Asia and the Pacific" which was offered by the women's studies program at the University of Hawai'i. The postdoctoral program offered me a unique opportunity to work with a group of scholars on this new topic. My thanks go not only to the host, the women's studies program at the University of Hawai'i, but also to the Rockefeller Fellows in this program.

Returning to China from the UK in 2004 to take up a position at Shanghai University offered me a chance to observe first-hand the development of feminist subjectivities in China at the dawn of the twenty-first century. Many thanks go to Wu Song, the former Vice President of Shanghai University, who supported me in setting up the Center for Gender and Cultural Studies so that my colleagues and I have a platform to carry on the work of women's and gender studies in the context of a severe academic situation in China.

My thanks also go to the EU Marie Curie International Incoming Fellowship within the Seventh European Community Framework Programme under the project "Cross-Cultural Encounters – The Travels of Gender Theory and Practice to China and the Nordic Countries", which supported me in writing up this book between 2013 and 2014. The Nordic Institute of Asia Studies (NIAS) at the University of Copenhagen provided an institutional home for the project. I would like to thank the University of Copenhagen and the director Dr Geir Helgesen and colleagues of NIAS Dr Cecilia Milwertz, Gerald Jackson, Inga-Lill Blomkvist, Katrine Herold and special consultant Solgerd Just Mikkelsen for all their kind help and generous support.

I would also like to thank those friends and colleagues who read the chapters of this book and gave me feedback on the long journey of the book's formation: Ruth Dawson, Kathy Ferguson, Mary John, Mary Madden, Monique Mironesco, Sheila Rinowbotham, Bo Ærenlund Sørensen, and Qi Wang.

I am grateful to Kathy Davis and Mary Evans, the editors of the series "The Feminist Imagination-Europe and Beyond", of which this is just one volume, for their insightful suggestions and great encouragement.

Several chapters of this book are based on previously published articles. I would like to thank the publishers of the following articles for their permission to use material which appears in the course of this book: Chapter 1: "Toward an Alternative Traveling Theory", in *Signs*, 39, 3 (Spring 2014), 584–592; Chapter 2: "Awakening Again: Travelling Feminism in China in the 1980s", in *Women's Studies International Forum*, 28, 4 (2005), 274–288; Chapter 3: "Duihua (Dialogue) In-Between: A Process of Translating the Term 'Feminism' in China", in *Interventions*, 9, 2 (2007), 174–193; and "'What About Other Translation Routes (East-West)?' The Concept of the Term 'Gender' Traveling into and throughout China", in Kathy E. Ferguson and Monique Mironesco, eds. *Gender and Globalization in Asia and the Pacific: Method, Practice, Theory*, Honolulu: University of Hawai'i Press (2008), 79–100.

I am very grateful to my commissioning editor at Ashgate Publishing, Neil Jordan, for his advice, guidance, and attention to detail in putting my book to bed.

Finally, my love and thanks go to my partner (by marriage), Allen Roberts, for literally travelling the whole journey with me, for endless reading, commenting, and correcting. I could not have finished this book without the patience and support that he gave me.

At this point, I must mention, with heavy sadness, the deaths of two international feminists, my friends Janet Melvin and Bao Xiaolan, whom I and others will greatly miss.

1 Introduction
How far does travelling theory travel? Questions for travelling theory and translation

This book is concerned with the question of why and how the ideas and knowledge of feminism travel from 'here' (the West) to 'there' (China). In what form and by whom has feminist theory and practice been sent, received, understood, and translated, or even rejected? I point to the impact of these travels; in particular, I focus on the 'travelling theory' and 'translation' of transnational feminist ideas and knowledge and the formulation of these ideas within Chinese women's and gender studies, discourse, and practices, together with the perceived status of Chinese agency in the mediated processes of 'translation' occurring from the 1980s up to the present day.

As an important part of postmodern thinking, 'travelling theory' has been discussed since the 1980s, with Edward Said's essay "Travelling Theory" (1984) being the centrally influential contribution on the topic. In this essay, Said discusses György Lukács (a participant in the struggle in the Hungarian Soviet Republic of 1919) as used by Lucien Goldmann (an expatriate historian at the Sorbonne after World War II), and then Goldmann as used by Raymond Williams (an English cultural studies scholar at Cambridge in the mid- to late twentieth century). Said emphasises two main points: first, that theories lose some of their original power and rebelliousness when they travel to other periods and new situations; second, that this implies processes of representation and institutionalisation different from those prevailing at the point of origin (Said, 1984).

Based on these patterns, Said also suggested the insightful approaches to thinking through travelling theories. He addresses the importance of a historical approach to theory and ideas, stressing that both a theory's origin and its later interpretation are of crucial importance. Proceeding from this historical approach, Said addresses the issue of 'misreading'. He finds the assumption that the borrowings and re-interpretations of theory *are* the misreading. Misreadings (as they occur) should be treated as part of the historical transmission of ideas and theories from one setting to another (Said, 1984: 236).

Indeed, theories are always on the move as Said pointed out, but when I tried to use Said's ideas to solve puzzles that I had with theory, his model of 'travelling theory' could not satisfactorily answer my questions. For example, the most influential feminist book of the second half of the twentieth century, Simone de Beauvoir's *The Second Sex*, was published in France in 1949, and although it sold well and provoked some outraged comments along with positive response in France, it did not trigger an intellectual revolution in other parts of the world. It was not until the mid-1960s and the so-called second wave of feminist discussion that the book, in its English language translation, was taken up and proclaimed to contain an earth-shattering analysis: Kate Millett, Ti-Grace Atkinson, and Shulamith Firestone, all authors of important works of 1960s feminist theory, dedicated their books to de Beauvoir. This transatlantic connection turned a French intellectual's book into a much wider feminist and political event (Braidotti, 1992). However, when *The Second Sex* travelled to China during the 1980s, quite a different story unfolded. This will be discussed in detail in a later chapter.

This example helps to reformulate my first set of questions about 'travel': Is there something inherently mobile in the nature of theory? If not, when, where, for whom and why do theories and ideas travel or not travel? Does feminist theory travel in the same way as other theories? Said's 'travelling theory' consigns these questions to silence.

If this is not the same thing as arguing that there is something mobile in the nature of theory, that means there must be some power that encourages (persuades) some theories to travel. What is this 'power'? Said put this question aside without giving a satisfactory answer.

Throughout contemporary Euro-American criticism from the late 1970s to the 1990s, a counter-concept of 'creolisation' or 'hybridity' has come to reflect what is often termed a 'postmodern turn' in cultural criticism (Kaplan, 1996). In his essay "Notes on Theory and Travel", James Clifford offers some interesting questions and comments on the idea of travelling theory. He argues that theory is no longer naturally 'at home' in the West, or more cautiously, that this privileged place is now increasingly contested, cut across by other locations, claims, and trajectories of knowledge articulating racial, gender, and cultural differences (Clifford, 1989: 179). Clifford also points out that Said's ideas about travelling theory need to be modified if they are to be extended to a postcolonial context. Its view of the Budapest, Paris, and London itinerary of theory is both linear and confined to Europe.

For Clifford, the metaphor of travel assists in de-essentialising both research and the subjects of research and it opens up a new field for discussion by problematising the conventional sense of the term. Nonetheless, Clifford's theoretical discourse assumes the utility and applicability of related metaphors, such as that of the hotel as 'a site of travel encounters' – terms which are not innocent. Thus bell hooks has argued that travel, as read in Clifford's work, is overdetermined and produced at the 'centre' of Western social and political power; she writes that

> holding on to the concept of 'travel' as we know it is also a way to hold on to imperialism.... Travel is not a word that can be easily evoked to talk about the Middle Passage, the Trail of Tears, the landing of Chinese immigrants, the forced relocation of Japanese-Americans, or the plight of the homeless.
> (Clifford, 1992: 173)

Some additional questions need to be asked concerning the travelling of theory, such as: Where and how are theories produced? And by whom and for what purposes?

Perhaps the most basic question that needs to be asked concerns what is meant by theory in Said's travelling theory. Said's ideas about travelling theory are derived from the high humanist traditions of comparative literature and philology which have shaped his critical method as well as his choice of texts. The assumption is, as Aijaz Ahmad points out, that Said's theory is Euro-American centred, and Said

> speaks of the West, or Europe, as the one which produces the knowledge, the East as the object of that knowledge. In other words, he seems to posit stable subject-object identities, as well as ontological and epistemological distinctions between the two.
> (Ahmad, 1992: 183)

In this case, theories from the East and South, from the periphery, have been excluded as theory and are simply not considered to be in the league of mainstream travelling theory to which Said belongs.

During the 1990s, transnational feminism voiced a powerful critique of travelling theory. A related issue here concerns power relationships, particularly what Foucault (1977) terms "power/knowledge", something simply ignored in Said's analysis of travelling theory. As Caren Kaplan points out:

> Euro-American poststructuralist and postmodern critical practices have been slow to acknowledge this transnational material context. The subject position of the critic (or the multiplicity of subject positions available to the critic) has not received significant attention, either dismissed as vulgar and essentialist 'identity politics' or erased through the Eurocentric rhetoric of universality. Nor has the 'travel' of theories and theorists been fully considered as part of the legacy of imperialism nor as part of the politics of cultural production in transnational modernities and postmodernities.
> (Kaplan, 1996: 103)

Therefore, the issue of the "politics of location", initially addressed by Adrienne Rich (1987), has subsequently been discussed by a number of post-colonial feminists and become a wide-ranging debate, linking with the global and the local in feminist inquiry.[1]

Furthermore, theories, especially feminist theory, do not just travel to and in academic circles; they also travel to larger social movements. What happens when they travel to and are accepted within society at large? The debates and research on transnational feminist praxis offer us even more important questions to consider when thinking about travelling theory.

Revisiting transnational feminism

Since the 1990s, the theories of *transnational feminism* have challenged the Eurocentric, colonialist perspective of knowledge production that disregards local knowledge and the power relations of travel as part of the knowledge production through which subjects are constituted. Focusing on the phenomenon of how feminism has flowed around the world, scholars of transnational feminism have argued that knowledge production takes place through multiple related contexts that acknowledge the roles played by and the interaction between different localities in the process of globalisation, and that flows of knowledge generate different meanings in different places (Grewal and Kaplan, 1994; Alexander and Mohanty, 1997). From this analytical perspective, feminisms in different places not only reflect but are also active and explicit participants in processes of globalisation, engaging with and producing cross-border cultural, political, and economic flows.

During the past two decades, feminist scholars studying the diversity of the geopolitical contexts of globalisation have focused their attention on the relations between feminist theories and practices. Some of them have followed the trail of travelling academic feminist theories and tried to understand their directions and their reception in distinctive political and cultural backgrounds.[2] Others have studied gender-based movements and have struggled to grasp mutual meanings in the conceptions of feminism that they have encountered, and have attempted to construct a strategy for movements.[3]

These feminist scholars have shown that feminist theory has flowed far more easily from North to South and from West to East (particularly from the United States to other parts of the world), whereas flows in other directions are nearly non-existent (Costa, 2000; Min, 2008; Thayer, 2010). In Europe, the hegemony of US feminist theory has been challenged (Davis and Evans, 2011). However, there are many other invisible discursive trajectories that link the development of feminist theories and movements around the world which have so far been ignored. The cross-regional interaction between China and the Nordic countries is one example of the effects of globalisation on transnational academic currents, yet there has been no (or very little) research into this important topic. The questions that have been asked have only scratched the surface and have thus failed to reveal some of the untold stories of the cross-regional flow of gender theory between China and the Nordic countries.[4]

In the context of China, feminists in the academy have been considering the power relationship between travelling theory and localisation since the late 1990s, when the asymmetrical distribution of knowledge was recognised. I wrote more than ten years ago that

> if debates about postmodernism and post-colonialism in women's studies in China are belated, then what other important feminist ideas have not yet travelled to China? For instance, works by women of colour (even Americans such as bell hooks, Gloria Anzaldua, Angela Davis) have not yet been heard nor read in China. Women's studies and feminism in Eastern Europe, the Middle East, India and Africa go almost unheard, not to mention Australian, Latin American feminism. . . . The power relationship behind this global flow of feminist ideas, publications and activism should be revealed and this is clearly one of the new areas of work that needs to be encouraged.
>
> (Min, 2002: 233)

If we map the routes by which transnational feminism has travelled to China over the past decade, we see that US feminist theories are still in the lead. During this period, the books of bell hooks, Alison Jagger, and Nancy Fraser have been translated into Chinese, as have those of Judith Butler, who was regarded the new star in China for a few years. However, is this not just another example of academic fashion determining (who and) what is hot and (who and) what is not? Or have some theories been translated and published without ever travelling? This will be explored later.

If we look at the field of social movements, it may come as a surprise that transnational links to development funding played a crucial role in pushing Chinese women's and gender studies into particular ways of connecting with the international community in the 1990s. The Ford Foundation played the most prominent role in the 1990s by funding the major women/gender studies conferences and seminars. In addition to significant women's studies projects on reproductive health in China, the Ford Foundation also funded projects on rural women's development, women's education, the mobility of the female population, women's legislation, and the women's and gender studies curriculum in higher education. Chinese women's and gender studies lacked funding resources within China, so relying on Western and international foundations was seen as the only option. In addition to funding, these foundations have also offered ideas of their own. Their support, which has been vitally important for many non-governmental organisations (NGOs) in China, was thus ideological as well as financial.[5]

Women's and gender studies scholars have noted that many of the projects, ideas, and funding come from abroad in the name of the 'international community'. However, we are mostly in the dark, or are reluctant to question, what role the terms 'gender', 'development', and 'NGO' play in the neoliberal development agenda, and how this discourse has ensured that gender has achieved a place within international social movements. No doubt this has happened because development regimes target women for special consideration (Harcourt, 2009, 2010).

Confronted with this situation, the epistemological alternative voiced by some scholars is that "there is no global justice without global cognitive justice" (Santos, 2006: 14). In other words, the development of alternative thinking is a crucial task for confronting the predominant knowledge production on globalisation and achieving global justice. This radical thinking will be the starting point for my new approach to travelling theory.

Constructing an alternative travelling theory

My approach to translation and travelling theory is to develop an alternative way of thinking about travelling theory, which criticises and expands upon the work of Said and others in order to develop an interdisciplinary methodology for analysing theories and their possibilities for travel. It will contribute innovative approaches in the following ways.

First, travelling theory usually focuses on the travellers, that is, the travelling theories. An alternative travelling theory will also take into account both the people in the places where the theories are received and how these people either welcome, adopt, or are suspicious of the theories that travel.

For the people in the places where theories are received, the questions should be: Where are these theories produced? Where do they come from? What is the relationship between geohistorical location and knowledge production? What are their local histories? How are such theories expressed when they travel through regional differences? Are the theories just repeated in the new environment, or do they face limits here?

Second, most literature on travelling theory deals with the discursive issue. An alternative travelling theory will include the study of the links between discursive and material conditions, which means it will study not only the written translations but also the practices that follow from translation and the interaction between discourse and practice.

The conditions for travelling theories have been profoundly changed by the globalisation of economy, society, and culture, and by the rapid development of technical communication and media. As Gudrun-Axeli Knapp points out, "The changing conditions of travelling theories cannot be tackled today without reflecting the recent development of a highly competitive capitalist world market" (Knapp, 2005: 251). With knowledge and information turning into highly valued commodities, with academic research and higher education dominated by the capitalist market, we are all under pressure to produce knowledge that sells (or buys).

The issue of the materiality of knowledge production in the transnational field has been addressed by transnational feminists. In the travels of feminist theories in the Americas, there are 'theory brokers' including academics, international and national donors, feminist NGOs, and grassroots women's organisations and movements for the production, circulation, and reception of feminisms (Alvarez, 2000; Thayer, 2010; Costa, 2014).

With the global flow of funding, there is also a rising "social movement market" (Thayer, 2010: 128). Movements and organisations trade their ideas, knowledge production, and skills in this market. The material reality of funding flows also has a powerful discursive dimension. In the 1980s, the Chinese state began to reduce its support for the women's liberation movement, and international development aid has become indispensable for the women's movement in some areas. Under these conditions, how can organisations manage? This poses a question to feminists North and South, East and West: how can we develop equal political relationships in the 'social movement market' without being affected by unequal conditions?

The importance of studying the links between discursive and material conditions, as Chandra Talpade Mohanty has pointed out, lies in the fact that

> the dissolving of the systemic analyses of women of color and transnational feminist projects into purely discursive (representation) analyses of ruptures, fluidity, and discontinuities symptomatic of poststructural critique contributes to a threshold of disappearance of materialist feminist projects that target the state and other governing institutions. It is this danger of the appropriation of radical women of color and transnational feminist projects that should be of deep concern to us all.
>
> (Mohanty, 2013: 986–987)

Third, an alternative travelling theory will explore the complexities of the relationship between power and influence that underpins what does and what does *not* travel. Why do some theories travel well, while other theories rarely or never travel? Why have some theories been translated into Chinese, but not travelled well? The inclusion of theories that do not travel is important for understanding both what does travel and, more broadly, the power relationship involved in cross-cultural exchanges.

We know that the international dimension of knowledge is characterised by a worldwide information flow that is increasingly facilitated by technology, but we are much less cognizant of the significant global gap in access to both producing and consuming knowledge. It may be that the division of labour in the international knowledge system is one of the most salient features of that system. Hans N. Weiler has revealed that this problem is similar to how

> key intellectual tasks, such as setting theoretical agendas and methodological standards, are the prerogative of a relatively small number of societies and institutions that play a disproportionately important role in this system – societies and institutions which are, almost without exception, located in the economically privileged regions of the world.
> (Weiler, 2009: 4)

They are mainly located in the United States and Western Europe; some are major institutions such as the UN and the World Bank, which wield considerable economic and political influence and subscribe to an orthodox system of knowledge. Any country or institution hoping to obtain financial support from the UN or the World Bank needs to master the appropriate discourse and language.

The dominance of the United States as a world power and the English language allow the United States easy access to resources, as well as determining what should be translated. For instance, the Chinese Society for Women's Studies (CSWS) was a very important element in the process of translating key works of gender theory into Chinese in the 1990s. Almost all of the literature translated by the CSWS originated in the United States. Therefore, an investigation into the political economy of knowledge production – the structures and the sets of power relations – needs to be undertaken.

Alternative travelling theory is my key methodology for analysing theories and their possibilities for travel. However, without the 'vehicle of translation', the travelling of theory cannot take place. As Lydia H. Liu notes:

> With the suppression of that vehicle, travel becomes such an abstract idea that it makes no difference in which direction theory travels (from West to East or vice versa) and for what purpose (cultural exchange, imperialism, or colonization?), or in which language and for what audience.
> (Liu, L., 1995: 21)

The issue of translation, a hidden set of power relations involved in the processes of travelling theory, must be addressed as part of the process of re-signification.

Are issues in translation also issues in knowing?

Since the end of the 1980s, I have been translating feminist theories and women's studies scholarship from English into Chinese. I always knew that it is not easy to translate academic work from one language to another, but I always strove for my translations to reach the standard summed up in the old Chinese saying: "Faithfulness, correctness and elegance" (信达雅). The question of translation did not occur to me until 1997, when two events occurred that caused me to think much more seriously about the issue. One was my involvement in discussions concerning the translation of an article on "Feminist Philosophy in China" from Chinese to English and back to Chinese. The article was written by Lin Chun, Liu Bohong, and Jin Yihong (1998). The first version of the article was written in Chinese and included a number of Chinese feminist viewpoints on women's studies in China. The English translation of the article adapted the concepts and writing style to better suit a Western audience. When this English version was translated back into Chinese, many Chinese women felt it no longer sounded Chinese.[6]

The other event that caused me to think more about translation was my involvement in two debates, in 1994 and 1997, over how to translate the term 'feminism' into Chinese; both debates involved the CSWS. In 1994, and 1997, the CSWS organised a group of its members to write and translate two books about Western feminism and women's studies, which it published in China. There was much discussion and debate among CSWS members via letters and emails about how to translate the term.[7] These two events made me realise that if we are to engage in a meaningful dialogue across languages and cultures, translation issues are crucial. Translation is neither just good or bad; there are some aspects beyond "faithfulness, correctness, and elegance", and I have had a keen interest in the topic of translation ever since.

Normally, anxiety about translation issues began with looking for the right words, noticing language barriers in current international feminist dialogue, and asking how to negotiate the shaping of meaning by political and cultural forces. My own interest concerns what it is that we should be anxious or concerned about when doing translation. Is translation just a matter of looking for the right words, or is there something going on beyond the words themselves? And if the latter, what precisely is this? What else do we know or can we say about translation and its implications for cross-cultural understanding? And indeed, what does it mean for a feminist scholar to cross the language barrier between two or more cultures and linguistic communities?

For me, the most exciting development in translation studies was that associated with "the cultural turn" (Lefevere and Bassnett, 1990). The turn to culture adds an important dimension to translation studies, shifting the key question away from "How should we translate and what is a correct translation?" to "What do translations do, how do they circulate in the world and elicit responses?"

More important still, how did the ensuing debates within translation studies view translation, not just as a process of transcoding but instead as an act of communication, as informed by the tensions involved in all cultural representation

(Snell-Hornby, 1990; Simon, 1996)? Translation has been seen as a highly manipulative activity that involves all kinds of stages in the process of transfer across linguistic and cultural boundaries (Bassnett and Trivedi, 2002).

In his seminal article on translation, Talal Asad brought the issue of translation, with its political and economic angles, to the table. He cites cultural translation as crucial in power relations around cross-cultural interpretation and suggests that closer attention should be paid to the social and political context. These ideas about cultural translation have, I think, some major implications for comparative scholarship and for cross-cultural studies. As Asad points out, translating into another language has less to do with linguistic competence and much more to do with institutional practices and the knowledge/power relationships which authorise certain ways of 'knowing' about other cultures:

> The reason for this is, first, that in their political-economic relations with Third World countries, Western nations have the greater ability to manipulate the latter. And second, Western languages produce and deploy *desired* knowledge more readily than Third World languages do.
>
> (Asad, 1986: 157–158)

Within these debates, there are some issues in translation that I want to focus on in particular. The first is the issue of *equivalence*. Translation involves the rendering of a source language (SL) text into a text in the target language (TL), so as to ensure that the surface meaning of the two will be approximately similar and the structures of the SL will be preserved as closely as possible (Bassnett, 1991). However, in order to find the right term in the TL, it is important to understand the culture of the original term, because its meaning is culturally based. However, the more extensive this embedding is, the more difficult it is to find equivalent terms and ideas from the other culture. Considering this problem involves thinking about the issue of equivalence. Equivalence has been described as 'a much-used and abused' term in translation studies, and contemporary translation studies scholars stress that equivalence in translation should not be approached as a search for *sameness* (Godard, 1990; Lefevere and Bassnett, 1990; Bassnett, 1991). This is because sameness cannot even exist between two TL versions of the same text, let alone between the SL and the TL version.

The second issue, following from this, is that of *cultural untranslatability*. There are two broad kinds of untranslatability: linguistic and cultural. The former comes about due to differences between the SL and the TL texts and is relatively straightforward; the latter is due to the absence in the TL culture of a relevant situational feature for the SL text, and is intellectually more intractable. But does this occur, as Catford (1967) claims, in a context in which more abstract terms such as 'democracy' cannot be seen as untranslatable owing to the fact that such terms are truly international and transferable across cultures? Bassnett disagrees, and argues that the reader will have a concept of such terms based on their own cultural context and will apply that particularised view accordingly (Bassnett, 1991: 33).

However, I want to go further than this and move the issue of cultural untranslatability into the reflective area of transnational feminist practice. Clearly, the intellectual history of the women's movement of the past 30 years shows that terms such as feminism and gender have been contested more often than they have been accepted; in the process of travelling and translation they have often been unwanted or even rejected. The untranslatability might have been used as a new method for people to construct new understandings for the terms. The issue of cultural untranslatability is clearly crucially important, and I shall go on to explore how it has featured in relation to transnational feminism, particularly to women's and gender studies in China.

The third important issue concerns the idea of *'faithful' and 'unfaithful' translations*. Translators used to think that 'good translation' meant that the original meaning would be preserved by the act of translation, and consequently their objective was to strive for faithful translation, where the target text would function in the target culture in the same way the source text had functioned in the source culture. However, "Translations are therefore not 'faithful' on the levels they have traditionally been required to be – to achieve 'functional equivalence' a translator may have to substantially adapt the source text" (Lefevere and Bassnett, 1990: 8). The issue of unfaithful or 'faithless' translation has arisen in translation studies, cultural studies and women's and gender studies, where some scholars have argued that translation must necessarily amount to faithless appropriation (Scott, Kaplan, and Keates, 1997: 2; Tsing, 1997: 254). This notion of unfaithful translation is one I find interesting because it can be used to shift our thinking: instead of trying to localise the original and analyse the faithfulness of the copies, translation should instead be redefined as a process of continual negotiation which can be investigated and analysed.

The fourth issue I raise centres on the *visibility of the translator*. If translation is no longer treated as an invisible practice, then the translator needs to step out of the shadows and be recognised as an active agent. Thus, the study of the intellectual role of translators has emerged as an important topic in translation studies, where increasing attention has been paid to their statements about translation. As Benjamin argued:

> A translation issues from the original – not so much its life as from its afterlife.... The concept of life is given its due only if everything that has a history of its own, and is not merely the setting for history, is credited with life.
> (Benjamin, 1973: 72)

Furthermore, translators not only help to give new life to the originals they translate; they also need to consider how to inject the kind of life they discern in the originals into their new target language version. In other words, the translators create an account or revision of the original, intended for a particular time and a particular readership (Lefevere, 1995: 7). In order to grant a text a new life, translators therefore need great skills and knowledge beyond the linguistic:

> The primary task of the translator is to translate not what is there but what is *not* there, to translate the implicit and the assumed, the blank spaces between words. The difficulty of doing this effectively is immense.
> (Bielsa and Bassnett, 2009: 6)

This reconception of translators is intimately linked with my previous notion of an alternative travelling theory.

How can we create a shared knowledge through translations? A more positive question for translation has been addressed by Boaventura de Sousa Santos. Rather than focusing on whether or not a particular concept or theory has been translated 'correctly' so as to maintain a certain essence, Santos (2006) offers a more positive way of viewing translation. He points out that the recognition of a diversity of understandings in different contexts may allow for fruitful dialogue. In this way translation allows for the recognition of different 'knowledges' and experiences of the world to become both available and possible. This idea of translation further permits the creation of new meanings and new directions by which shared knowledges will be produced.

There remains, though, the question of how to make knowledge shared through translation. In order to answer this question, Santos proposes a continuous process of translating the concern for dignity between the Western concept of human rights, the Islamic concept of *umma* (community), and the Hindu concept of *dharma* (cosmic harmony involving human and all other beings) (Santos, 1999, 2006). In terms of translation, he points out:

> In sum, the work of translation in the intercultural contact zone among movements/organizations expounding different conceptions of human dignity allows us to identify the fundamental weakness of Western culture as consisting in dichotomizing too strictly between the individual and society, thus becoming vulnerable to possessive individualism, narcissism, alienation and anomie. On the other hand, the fundamental weakness of Hindu and Islamic culture lies in the fact that they both fail to recognize that human suffering has an irreducible individual dimension, which can only be adequately addressed in a society not hierarchically organized.
> (Santos, 2006: 135–136)

This is a radical view of translation, quite unlike the conventional view of translation which has regarded Europe and the United States to be the great originals and reduced the rest of world to the state of copying – a view that has held translations in lesser regard than originals because translations were regard as a type of copy. Therefore, "It is important also to remember that the language of 'loss' has featured so strongly in many comments on translation" (Bassnett and Trivedi, 2002: 4). Bassnett and Trivedi posed important questions, such as:

> So how were the colonies, emerging from colonialism, to deal with that dilemma? How might they find a way to assert themselves and their own culture, to reject the appellative of 'copy' or 'translation' without at the same time rejecting everything that might be of value that came from Europe?
> (Bassnett and Trivedi, 2002: 4)

For Santos, the recognition of reciprocal incompleteness and weakness is an essential condition of cross-cultural dialogue. The work of translation depends both on identification of incompleteness and weakness and on its trans-local intelligibility. Translation, then, is a process of cross-cultural dialogue in a more equal setting.

However, the key issues of translation – such as being faithful or unfaithful, 'losing' and 'gaining', and 'Who is the translator?' – have been addressed by scholars of post-colonial and feminist translation studies since the 1980s. Indeed, the issues of translation have become an important domain in the process of globalisation. Following this line, I agree that

> the question of translation becomes quite pertinent and constitutes a unique space from which, on the one hand, to take on critical analyses of representation and power and the asymmetries between languages and, on the other, to examine the knowledge formations and institutionalities in/through which these theories and concepts travel.
> (Costa, 2014: 20)

As we have seen, transnational feminists have not only played an important part in translation practices, but they have also pointed to important questions and contributed research on this topic.[8]

Translation is a unique way of understanding the knowledge production of transnational feminism, or for that matter any transnational 'ism'.

About the book

The immense diversity of gender and women's studies in China needs to be recognised and therefore this book will focus on a few concepts such as feminism, gender, and NGO, which came travelling to China in the 1980s, 1990s, and 2000s. This book also includes case studies of three different organisations that came into existence at different times and reflect different 'parts' of China.

These are the All China Women's Federation (ACWF), the Yunnan Reproductive Health Research Association (YRHRA), and the overseas Chinese Society for Women's Studies (CSWS). The particular focus is on the detailed everyday events and exchanges by which transnational feminism travels.

To capture the pertinent particulars of the topics mentioned earlier, I have systematically examined information from Chinese and English language materials, including Chinese women's studies journals, books, and relevant conference papers. I also conducted interviews during my fieldwork in China in 1999 and 2003 from various Chinese women's studies scholars and cadres from the Women's Federation. My involvement in the place-based, collaborative project "Women and Development Project Design, Analysis, and Implementation" in Xian and Kunming since 2002 has given me valuable hands-on experience in observing one of the routes by which the term gender travels. Returning to China from the UK in 2004 to take up a position at Shanghai University offered me a chance to observe first-hand the development of feminist subjectivities in China at the dawn of the twenty-first century.

Chapter 1 is the introduction of this book. My approach to travelling theory and translation is to develop an alternative way of thinking about travelling theory which criticises and expands upon the work of Said and others in order to develop an interdisciplinary methodology – alternative travelling theory – for analysing transnational feminism within Chinese women's and gender studies, discourse and practices.

Chapter 2 of this book is concerned with travelling feminism during the 1980s. In exploring this complex subject, I will start my journey from the point of departure and follow the route via which information related to feminism and women's studies travelled. By taking up one of the major feminist works that travelled to China – Simone de Beauvoir's *The Second Sex* – I hope to illustrate that the intellectual history involved in this process was far more complex and ambiguous than previously assumed. Finally, I will look at the development of theorising about women in China.

Chapter 3 discusses the encounters of feminism and gender as travelling concepts in mainland China. In the years immediately after the Beijing Conference of 1995, a major debate revolved around asking whether the term feminism was meaningful for Chinese women at all, but this later shifted to a concern over how to translate the term. However, the story of the term gender travelling to China is quite different, and in a political sense it has had a much easier journey than the term feminism. Three different kinds of translator were central during the 1980s and the 1990s to shaping the dialogue on feminism: the official state-sponsored women's organisation, the ACWF, headquartered in Beijing; Chinese women's studies scholars and activists living in mainland China; and the CSWS, based in the United States, whose email discussions have included diverse opinions and viewpoints from other parts of the world. My discussion is linked in a critical way to debates about transnational feminism and translation.

Chapters 4 and 5 will convey some of the concerns of this exciting time in Chinese feminism by tracing the emergence of different attitudes and approaches toward transnational feminisms in the Women's Federation and in academic circles in the 1990s. The focus will be on attitudes towards what in Chinese is termed *jiegui* (linking up with the international track) among different groups of Chinese women, by discussing the narratives of women's studies scholars and activists and the ACWF. I shall also examine why and how particular travelling theories and concepts, such as gender and NGO, travelled into Chinese women's studies circles and beyond. Furthermore, I will look at the new trend of 'doing a project' and focus on the processes involved therein by probing various case studies. In Chapter 4, I shall scrutinise travelling theory by looking at stories involving two key players: the CSWS and the YRHRA, both of which have been involved in many research projects since the 1990s.

Finally, Chapter 6 will focus on the most recent decade, where economic growth–focused development became further intensified in China and state-organised capitalism developed. One of the consequences of this development was to widen the social-gender gap and hence increase gender inequality. As a result, diverse and multidimensional feminisms have emerged between the global and the local in China. I propose to chart not only the success stories of transnational feminisms, but also the disturbing junctures of dealing with the demands of neoliberalism and the new conservatism. The desire to *jiegui* with transnational feminism produced a need to rethink the homogenised dichotomies of West and East, local and global. The desire to re-root feminism in local narratives of inequality resulted in a need to revisit another period of unfinished social revolution: the era of state socialism. Finally, the desire to extend more equal citizenship rights created a new women's movement.

Notes

1 See Grewal and Kaplan (1994); Kaplan (1996); Friedman (1998); Costa (2000); Mohanty (2003); Davis (2007); and Swarr and Nagar (2010).
2 For example, John, Mary E. (1996), *Discrepant Dislocations*, Berkeley, Los Angeles and London: University of California Press; de Lima Costa, Claudia (2000), "Being Here and Writing There: Gender and the Politics of Translation in a Brazilian Landscape", *Signs*, 25 (3), pp. 727–760; Knapp, Gudrun-Axeli (2005), "Race, Class, Gender: Reclaiming Baggage in Fast Travelling Theories", *European Journal of Women's Studies*, 12(3), pp. 249–265; Min, Dongchao (2008), "'What About Other Translation Routes (East-West)?' The Concept of the Term 'Gender' Traveling into and throughout China". In *Gender and Globalization in Asia and the Pacific: Method, Practice, Theory*, ed. Kathy E. Ferguson and Monique Mironesco, 79–100, Honolulu: University of Hawai'i Press.
3 For example, Ghodsee, Kristen (2004), "Feminism-by-Design: Emerging Capitalisms, Cultural Feminism, and Women's Nongovernmental Organizations in Postsocialist Eastern Europe", *Signs*, 29 (3), pp. 725–753; Liu, Dongxiao (2006), "When Do National Movements Adopt or Reject International Agendas?: A Comparative Analysis of the Chinese and Indian Women's Movements", *American Sociological Review*, 71 (6), pp. 921–942; Liu, Meng; Hu, Yanhong and Liao, Minli (2009), "Traveling Theory in China: Contextualization, Compromise and Combination", *Global Networks*, 9 (4), pp. 529–554;

Thayer, Millie (2010), *Making Transnational Feminism: Rural Women, NGO Activists, and Northern Donors in Brazil*, New York: Routledge.

4 For instance, there is the series of Sino-Nordic Women's and Gender Studies Conferences. Five conferences have been held in China and the Nordic countries since 2002. The topics have included globalisation, human rights and transnational feminism, among others. However, how far these theories have travelled into each region's women's and gender studies regional programmes and feminist movements warrants further study.

5 The situation with regard to funding has been changing over the past few years. For instance, the National Social Science and Humanities Research Fund has supported projects related to gender and women's issues since the early twenty-first century and the number of funded projects has increased every year.

6 More detail about the repercussions of this article in Chinese women's studies circles was provided in Ferguson (1997). The final version, "China", was published in Alison M. Jaggar and Iris Marion Young (eds) (1998), *A Companion to Feminist Philosophy*, Oxford: Blackwell.

7 I will discuss this case in Chapter 3.

8 See Davis, Kathy (2007), *The Making of Our Bodies, Ourselves: How Feminism Travels across Borders*, Durham and London: Duke University Press; Thayer, *Making Transnational Feminism*; Alvarez, Sonia E.; De Lima Costa, Claudia; Feliu, Veronica; Hester, Rebecca J.; Klahn, Norma and Thayer, Millie (eds) (2014), *Translocalities/Translocalidades: Feminist Politics of Translation in the Latin/a Americas*, Durham and London: Duke University Press.

2 Awakening again
The 1980s

> If the collective consciousness of Chinese women were awakened, then we would definitely see enlightened women actively involved in society, and would see self-improvement and consciousness-raising movements for women. In the painful process of weaning themselves away from society, Chinese women can learn to draw nurturing and strength from women themselves. In the face of traditional theory that has lost its efficacy, they can explore and choose new theories for women. At the same time, they can also choose 'organisation': new women's groups with various structures or with no structure could come into being one after another. Thus would we find a way toward collective female development even in the difficult organisational predicament of no way out.
>
> (Li, X., 1994a: 382)

Setting the scene

In China, the period from 1979 to 1989 has been described using the metaphor of spring, with associated terms such as 'thawing' and 'awakening'. Emerging from the unforgiving 'political winter' of the Cultural Revolution, Chinese society has been thought of as reviving the diversity and vigour that had been harshly repressed by the revolutionary-totalitarian regime. Departing from the Maoist version of socialism, which saw social change more in terms of class struggle than industrial expansion and technological innovation, Deng Xiaoping's leadership focused on the Four Modernisations of agriculture, industry, science and technology, and national defence. China now sees itself as having entered into a new era of modernisation. In the new period, progress and modernity once again serve as the ideals underpinning the notion of cultural production subscribed to by the country's elite intellectuals. Chinese intellectuals thus once again face the dilemma of nationalism and (the supposedly Western notion of) modernity, namely, how to determine what constitutes legitimate knowledge about Chinese identity.

Chinese intellectuals in the May Fourth Movement of 1919 adopted a Western view of history and used the term 'awakening' to mean that Chinese women should break from the traditional Confucian, and highly unequal, social relations between men and women. As the political and cultural echoes of the May Fourth Movement reverberated in the 1980s, the modernised West was once again identified as the model for linear, progressive, and democratic history and culture, and China was seen as epitomising a conservative and traditional culture. 'Awakening' was used to signal that Chinese women's collective consciousness should be roused from the benighted gender consciousness characteristic of Chinese society.

Just as modernisation travelled to China from the West and played an active role in political life in the early decades of the twentieth century, so too did feminism travel to China where it became part of the attempt to reform China into a modern country.[1] The kind of Cultural Revolution advocated by the May Fourth Movement, especially the idea of breaking with traditional notions of gender, was applauded by some intellectuals, but it was not supported in wider circles of society. As the Chinese feminist movement enjoyed little popular support, it was not surprising that it lost its momentum when the May Fourth Movement fell apart. After this, China's women's movement took a very different direction, seeking women's liberation through socialist struggle.

After 1949, the success of the socialist revolutionary movement meant that Chinese women saw their lives change remarkably, with formal equality introduced in the area of law and policy. Mao's well-known saying, "What men can do, women can do", encapsulated the ideology of gender equality from the 1950s to the 1970s, and gender inequalities in public institutions and ideology were, to a great extent, eliminated.

It was not until the mid-1980s that a collective consciousness that might be described as feminist arose among Chinese women. Women's studies as a research subject also came into being, especially in the All China Women's Federation (ACWF)[2] and within academic circles. At this time there was no women's movement comparable to what there had been in Western countries from the 1960s to the 1980s, so how do we account for the emergence of feminism and women's studies in China? Scholars working inside and outside of China have sought to answer this question, and they broadly agree that this new development was enabled by two parallel processes: a significant retreat of the state and a rapid expansion of the market.[3]

Overall, the post-1978 economic reforms had two consequences, which proved vital for the emergence of the new knowledge which came to be known as women's studies. First, the reforms brought a socio-economic transformation under which China switched from state socialism to market socialism, but this occurred in a way that eroded some of the policies which had been introduced to ensure equality for women, and therefore Chinese women became more vulnerable in the newly emerging labour market. Unfortunately, women were more frequently turned into sexual objects, and they were exploited and discriminated against in employment contexts. It was the increasing recognition of gender differences and inequalities that provided the impetus for establishing women's studies in China. Second, the reforms also opened up opportunities for women's self-awareness and self-organisation to thrive in autonomous spheres outside the state's control. Crucial in this regard was the 'movement towards the liberation of thought' which followed the Cultural Revolution and inspired many Chinese intellectuals. Humanism re-emerged in the 1980s, and enlightenment modernity, individual subjectivity, science, and universalism were introduced into various cultural and intellectual spaces. All of this helped encourage women's self-awareness. The impact first became apparent in the late 1970s in the work of young female writers. Many of the women's problems discussed in these writings resonated with the experiences of intellectuals and encouraged female scholars to examine gender issues in their respective fields. "Equality between men and women", which had been a central tenet of traditional socialist ideology, was for the first time questioned and challenged.

It has been argued that this approach to gender equality was an exploitative one: by postulating equality between men and women, it deprived women of their difference, rather than affirming difference as well as equality (Liu, L., 1993). Moreover, this interpretation of equality took men's behaviour to be the standard and thus left intact the low degree of self-awareness of Chinese women (Min, 1997). Furthermore, Chinese women achieved entry into the domain of production, but not into the production of public discourse, which was reserved for the state. Although state discourse granted women a central position, the language used to do so undermined women's self-identity and gender consciousness (Yang, 1999). There was a massive contradiction in the state's approach to gender equality. While the communist regime succeeded in weaving women into the new economic and social fabric, it also reinforced the political dependence of women upon the state. After all, the state did not establish a democratic system for individual rights, either for men or for women. Indeed, women's liberation, as well as social liberation in general, was profoundly circumscribed (Lin, C., 1997; Wang, Q., 1999).

These independent women's voices diverged from the general tone of state feminism, although most of them occupied positions within the state, and many of them were either scholars employed by state-run universities and research institutes or worked for the Women's Federation as cadres and researchers. It has also been suggested that the voices of these women differed from the male oppositional discourse, because "women intellectuals and professionals use their State positions to support feminist activities not initiated by the State and speak of feminist concerns, without at the same time furthering the ends of the party" (Yang, 1999: 57).

One of the initial challenges for women's studies in China was that with its introduction came a resurgence of interest among women in the women's movement of the May Fourth Movement and a desire to reconnect with an interrupted tradition following four decades of socialist state feminist discourse that failed to emphasise the male-female binary (Li, X., 1988; Meng and Dai, 1989). Certainly without the re-emphasis of the differences between men and women and the use of these to justify inequalities that came with economic reform, Chinese women would not have been propelled into increased self-awareness, and as a consequence women's studies would not have developed.

The first National Conference on Theoretical Research on Women, organised by the ACWF together with several universities and research institutes, took place in 1984 and addressed the social impact of economic reform on all aspects of women's work and lives. The conference led to the establishment of associations of women's studies on various levels in every province throughout the country. Because the new associations had the backing of the official and powerful ACWF, they mushroomed on various levels in every province through the 1980s. Members of the associations came from local Women's Federations (WFs) and also included academic scholars. This enabled women researchers and women activists to join forces and provided a platform for exchanging ideas, organising workshops, and publishing papers.

By the 1980s, the state and its ideologies no longer dominated intellectual space to the same extent as they previously had. How, then, did new ideas, unfamiliar concepts, and the free thinking of feminism emerge from and, in turn, influence the Chinese women's movement of the 1980s? Where did these new ideas come from? Which ideas and concepts were involved? How and why did the knowledge of women's studies and feminism travel to China? Who were the key people involved in promoting and theorising the particular knowledge that was travelling at this initial stage? What were the specific intellectual trends that stimulated Chinese women's studies activists and scholars and thus helped to stimulate their own free thinking?

In working through these questions, I will start my 'journey' from the point of departure and retrace the route via which information on feminism and women's studies travelled during the 1980s. By examining one major feminist's work – Simone de Beauvoir's *The Second Sex* – that travelled to and then within China, I shall show that the intellectual history involved in this process was far more complex and ambiguous than first assumed. Moving on, I will investigate the development of the 'theorising theory' of women in China. For this, I shall need to travel back to the Chinese women's studies circles of the 1980s, tracing the activities and viewpoints of the pioneers among the women's studies scholars and activists who were involved at the initial stage of 'travelling feminism'.

Departures

Before the post-1978 reforms there had been little communication between women in China and women in the West, and both remained enclosed in their own frameworks of ideas. The new 'open door' policy in China made it possible for Western feminist scholars to visit China, and Chinese women scholars gained the chance, for the first time since 1949, to travel to Western countries. These Chinese women brought back with them a range of Western feminist works and ideas, and they began the initial cross-cultural and political dialogues. (What this consisted of will be discussed in more detail later.)

To understand the way this new information about feminism, women's studies, and the ideas associated with these various groups were received, it must be remembered that feminist ideas travelled to China from the West, and most of them in the English language; consequently, these new ideas initially travelled through academic spaces. The term 'women's studies' first entered Chinese academic discourse in 1982 in a book review by Shirai Atsushi, "Women's Studies and the History of Women's Movements", published in *Studies of Social Sciences Abroad* (see Wan, 1988). Foreign literature studies was a pioneering subject, receiving and debating feminism in academic circles. For instance, feminist books such as Virginia Woolf's *A Room of One's Own* (1929), Simone de Beauvoir's *The Second Sex* (1969), Betty Friedan's *The Feminine Mystique* (1963), and Sandra Gilbert and Susan Gubar's *The Madwoman in the Attic* (1979) were introduced in 1983 (see Lin, S., 1995). Following this, also in the 1980s, a number of feminist books and articles were translated into Chinese, including *The Second Sex* and *The Feminine Mystique*. (In fact, these two books were the major feminist works discussed in Chinese women's studies circles in the 1980s.) From 1980 to 1983, according to Lin Shuming, five articles were published each year that introduced Western feminist literature theory into China; this number increased steadily, reaching 20 in 1988 and 32 in 1989. In 1989, *Feminist Literary Theory: A Reader*, edited by Mary Eagleton (1986), was the first Western feminist book of literary theory to be translated and published in Chinese (Lin, S., 1995).

Pioneering women's studies organisations in academic circles were set up where there were frequent cultural and academic exchanges between China and other countries, at places such as the Beijing Foreign Language Institute, Peking University, and Fudan University in Shanghai. The Centre for Women's Studies at Hangzhou University was typical of this development. This university maintained exchange scholarships with more than 30 foreign universities, and visiting scholars intending to study abroad regularly inquired if there was a centre for women's studies at the particular university they were interested in visiting. These enquiries led women scholars at several universities to realise that women's studies ought to be part of the academic mainstream, and so they encouraged universities to set up such centres in 1989 (Tong, 1993).

It was, however, not easy to find support from the traditional academy to establish women's studies as a discipline. The first obstacle to confront was the underestimation of this subject by mainstream academics. Qi Wenying, a professor of history at Peking University, describes the establishment of women's studies at the university in the following way:

> I was in the first group of intellectuals who went abroad after the Cultural Revolution in 1979. My research interest was American History, but I found that the subjects of women's studies and women's history existed during my visit to America! It was great to know that there was really a subject involving research on women. I was so excited. I met some people and bought some books on women's studies during this trip and wanted to introduce this subject to China. I came back to China in 1981. When I was reporting my trip to America at the meeting in the Department of History, I emphasised that we should develop the subject of women's history at our department.
>
> (Cai, Wang, and Du, 1999: 55)

Unfortunately, Professor Qi received no support from mainstream academic circles at that time. However, she and a group of female scholars continued to apply pressure and provide inspiration. Eventually, the department started teaching women's studies courses in 1984, and in 1988 a Women's Salon was formed at the university. In recalling the process of establishing the Centre for Women's Studies at Peking University, the director, Professor Zheng Bijun, thought that obtaining information on Western feminism was one of the crucial factors:

> One was a group of Chinese scholars who went abroad, such as Qi Wenying (Department of History), Tao Jie (Department of English). They brought back information on women's studies and Western feminism. Another factor was the lectures on women's studies by the foreign scholars. This had started during 1984 at the Department of English. Professor Qi Wenying had invited scholars to lecture in the Department of History also.
>
> (interview, Min/Zheng, 4/3/1999)

With increasing academic information from the West, and the major changes occurring in Chinese society, mainstream academics felt that they had to respond to this new situation. In 1988 I taught at Tianjin Normal University, and the chair of the university's Department of History and I discussed the subject of women's studies, which I was already involved in at the time. He had come across women's studies while in the UK as a visiting scholar in 1986, and he had heard that women's studies was considered an important part of the curriculum in many universities around the world. He thought that women's studies should also be an important part of the Chinese academic curriculum, and he asked me to teach the subject as an optional class in the Department of History at Tianjin Normal University. I taught this class for four years until I went to the UK as a visiting scholar in 1992.

How to obtain information on women's studies beyond what could be learned from the 'big names' was perhaps the other major obstacle we had to grapple with. At this early stage, our perceptions of Western feminism were shaped by personal contacts with Western feminists. For example, Li Xiaojiang, one of the translators of *The Second Sex*, had obtained the English version of this book from an American student in 1984. In the same year, a friend of a friend brought Betty Friedan's *The Feminine Mystique* back to China from the UK (interview, Min/Li, X., 3/3/1999). In one of her books she recalls the difficulty of getting Western materials in the 1980s:

> If I wanted to read a Western book (in English), I had to travel to Beijing. I did this twice a year, which became like a journey of pilgrimage. I spent days in the Beijing Library reading and photocopying *Signs* and *Women's Studies International Forum*, which were the only two feminist journals in the Library at that time.
>
> (Li, X., 1995: 12)

Thus, personal networks were an important factor in the shaping and channelling of information. Professor Sun Xiaomei, from the University of Chinese Women,[4] talked about this in the following way:

> When I started teaching the course on international women's history at this college in 1983, it was very difficult to get information on women from abroad. My mother was working at Xinhua News Agency, and she helped me to collect some information, so I was able to write an article on Third World women and had it published. It was an encouragement to me, but at that time, because of the political situation, I did not dare to write an article on Western women. In 1985, the ACWF sent delegates to the UN Third Women's Conference, and the head of the ACWF wanted us to pay more attention to women from abroad. In order to get information on the UN Conference, our college had to buy it from the Xinhua News Agency.
>
> (interview, Min/Sun, 9/3/1999)

I experienced some of the same problems as Professor Sun. When I started writing my book, *The International Women's Movement, 1789–1989* (Min, 1991), there was very little information on this subject in China. In the end I managed to acquire ten books, published in English on the women's movement from the Capital Library in Beijing through interlibrary loan, and that was all that was available on this subject. Of course, it was far less than I needed in order to write the book, so I wrote to friends living abroad when I needed additional information. They forwarded a great deal in the way of books and articles from the United States, Canada, Denmark, and Taiwan.

There were very few Chinese translations of Western feminist texts because most women's studies scholars who studied Chinese history or Chinese literature did not use foreign-language texts. Therefore, the feminist ideas that travelled to these scholars needed translation to enable Chinese academic study.

Sometimes, Western feminist ideas travelled via other places and/or spaces. Sheng Ying, one of the leading scholars on women's literature, told me that

> in order to get more information on Western feminism during the 1980s, I had to read Chinese publications which contained articles on feminist literary criticism from Hong Kong or Taiwan, such as the Hong Kong journal *Chinese and Foreign Literature*.
>
> (interview, Min/Sheng, 17/2/2001)

Sometimes, Chinese women's studies scholars received Western feminist information through lectures given by colleagues. For instance, one of my colleagues, Professor Du Fangqin, director of the Centre for Women's Studies at Tianjin Normal University, told me:

> In fact I haven't read *The Second Sex* properly. I heard about de Beauvoir's ideas from your women's studies classes rather than reading her book. . . . Perhaps I have a fear of reading the writings of Western people. I haven't read a lot of Western books on literature and history, because as soon as I started to read I would fall asleep. For me, reading Western feminist writings is a rather difficult thing.
>
> (interview, Min/Du, 7/4/1999)

'Reading' feminism through intermediary means such as publications from Hong Kong and Taiwan, or lectures by colleagues, made things easier for them. However, conducting research with the limited information about transnational feminisms available to us meant that the issue of translation remained a silent question in Chinese women's studies circles. Translation, as I see it, is never something carried out by a totally free and unfettered subject; instead it needs to be understood in relation to the constraints and possibilities of particular times and places.

Initially, not only was information about women's studies in short supply, but communication between the West and China was also full of misunderstandings and conflict. A Chinese feminist scholar, Dai Jinhua, had some interesting experiences in this respect:

> In the middle of the 1980s, I participated in a conference in which the participants were both Chinese and Western women. The Western women were feminists and they emphasised sisterhood. They were talking about

their experiences as women and the process of consciousness raising. Although they were very genuine, we thought they were quite naïve. After talking to us, they expected the Chinese women to respond in the same way about themselves. The Chinese women watched and listened sympathetically and said 'How sad for you! We haven't these kinds of problems'. The Chinese delegates realised that Western women were still having to fight for rights regarding divorce, equal pay, and so on. We had solved these problems ages ago. This was a very typical scene. We supposed that women's issues in China and in the West were totally different, that Western feminist theory was totally irrelevant to the Chinese situation.

(Dai, 1999: 143–144)

At the official level, an ACWF cadre, Xie Lihua, editor-in-chief of the journal *Farming Women Know It All* (*Nongjianü Baishitong*), has commented that in their first encounter with a Spanish women's group in 1985, she and her colleagues were shocked and dumbfounded when the Spanish leader described how her group promoted the 'sexual pleasure movement' and declared that women should have the same sexual rights as men, and that it was not only men who should gain enjoyment from sex. "At the time", Xie said, "it was like hearing an alien voice from the moon. We could not engage in exchange, or any meaningful dialogue. All we could do was nod our heads, with blank looks on our faces" (Xie, 1995: 51).

We need to remember that China had had 'closed doors' to the outside world for more than 20 years. During this time, Chinese women did not know what was happening in the outside world, and the outside world knew very little of what life was like for Chinese women. Indeed, travelling to each other's worlds was a difficult process, but it was necessary.

At the point of departure – that is, as women's studies research began to open up – those of us who were involved welcomed the retreat of the state because these changes fostered new possibilities for political action. Although we only had access to a limited amount of information on women's studies and feminist ideas, some dialogue did occur between Western feminist scholars and Chinese women. We started to travel to each other's worlds, and we were willing to understand each other. Although the journeys were full of translation, interpretation, and misunderstanding, the meetings still promoted women's studies by enabling Chinese women to make use of their foreign experiences.

Enlightening the enlighteners

Simone de Beauvoir's *The Second Sex* and Betty Friedan's *The Feminine Mystique* have been seen as inaugurating the second wave of feminism, a new feminism that bore the imprint of women activists of the New Left, a left that cannot not be confined to Marxist or socialist groupings. It is interesting to note that these two books have often been held up as symbols of how women's studies in China has been influenced by ideas from Western feminism, and several articles have stressed how influential these books were during the 1980s (Li and Zhang, 1994; Lin, S., 1995; Du, 1996; Min, 1997; Wang, 1997a). It is, however, rare to find discussion of any specific feminist ideas derived from these two books during the 1980s, and even in the 1990s they were only discussed in a very limited number of articles (see Tian, 1991; Rong, 1994; Li, X., 1999a, 2000a). As *The Second Sex* remains more popular than *The Feminine Mystique* in China, I will present a close reading of the book to discuss its impact in China during the 1980s. The questions of interest are: Did this book really have such an impact on Chinese women's studies as we are led to believe? If so, who actually read it, and what specific ideas were derived from it? What light is thrown on travelling theory by this book? How can we move beyond simple assumptions about impact and influence and instead develop a more grounded assessment of how the work travelled and with what result?

My claim is that although *The Second Sex* was translated into Chinese during the 1980s, it has had far less influence in China than previously assumed. According to Li Xiaojiang:

> For Chinese mass readers, the influence of this book is not its content, but its title. The earliest published copy in mainland China came from Taiwan. The translator of the book had changed the title to *Woman (nuren)—the Second Sex*.... At that time, the Cultural Revolution had just finished. This book was appearing in some bookstores along with some political books and pornographic magazines. The word 'woman' (nuren) appeared impressive. It was like a challenge to our society, in which woman had got lost in 'men and women are the same'.
>
> (Li, X., 1999a: 98)

Another Chinese writer, Dai Qing, makes a similar point regarding the title of de Beauvoir's book:

> What readers see is sex and not feminism (laughs). My feeling is that Chinese people are quite ignorant about things going on in Western post-industrial societies, things like homosexuality and feminism.
>
> (Wang, Z., 1993: 193)

If these views represent general impressions of this book, what was its impact on Chinese women's studies scholars and activists? According to Li Xiaojiang, de Beauvoir's book 'enlightened' us, the 'enlighteners' (interview, Min/Li, X., 3/3/1999). But how and in what ways were ideas gained from it; indeed, *were* any ideas gained from it?

With hindsight, and like millions of women in the world, I think that the most important thought that Chinese women's studies has gained from *The*

Second Sex is that "one is not born, but rather becomes, a woman" (de Beauvoir, 1969: 9). As my colleague Du Fangqin said:

> To be frank with you, I haven't paid much attention to the content of *The Second Sex*, but it doesn't mean I haven't been affected by it. I was inspired by 'One is not born, but rather becomes, a woman'. I don't know what it said in the original French, but the translation spread far and wide in China and we have gained much from it.... *The Second Sex* offered us the enlightenment, but not the theories or practical methods at that time.
>
> (interview, Min/Du, 7/4/1999)

The influence of this sentence was not only found in academic circles, but also in the Women's Federation. Sun Xiaomei, who taught cadres of the Women's Federation during the 1980s, commented:

> I cited this sentence from *The Second Sex* in my class, but there were so many Women's Federation old-liners in my class, I had to change the way I talked about it. I tried to discuss it around the issues facing Chinese women.
>
> (interview, Min/Sun, 9/3/1999)

Liu Bohong, the deputy director of the Institute of Women's Studies in the ACWF, said during one of our conversations, "de Beauvoir's 'One is not born, but rather becomes, a woman' impressed me very much, and her life experience had a strong appeal for me" (interview, Min/Liu, 4/3/1999). I had similar responses when I read *The Second Sex* in the late 1980s. Already personally involved in the newly developing women's studies movement at that time, it was the first Western feminist book that was available to read. After this first reading of the work of de Beauvoir, I was intent on reading all of her writings, including her autobiographies. I was fascinated by her feminist ideas as well as by her lifestyle.

In China, people of my generation did not have much choice about how we lived our everyday lives before the 1980s. Everyone was expected to marry at around 25 years of age and to have one child. If you were over 25 and still single, your family and other people would say that you had a 'personal problem'. For instance, in an interview with Janet Melvin and Diana Kingsbury in the early 1990s, I commented:

> People in most other countries can choose the lifestyle they like. You're not limited to only one way, the way everyone else is taking. But few people in China understand this. You're freer because you can decide for yourselves what kind of life you want. We Chinese have very few choices.
>
> (interview, Melvin and Kingsbury/Min, 4/1991)

For me, de Beauvoir's *The Second Sex* was less important than her autobiographies. Her feminism was less a set of ideas forming part of a political movement than it was a guide to living. For the first generation of Chinese women after 1949 who became feminists, de Beauvoir's life was truly seen as exemplary and was explored for clues about how we might live and engage with society. De Beauvoir's books and her life provided a model of what it might mean to be independent, intellectual, and female. This had a considerable impact on me and on other contemporary female academics who had read her work in detail.

De Beauvoir's declaration – "One is not born, but rather becomes, a woman" – particularly inspired me to rethink the process of becoming a woman in the Chinese context. How did we 'become' women during the period from 1949 to the end of the Cultural Revolution in a so-called equal, socialist society? I addressed this question in my women's studies classes at Tianjin Normal University from 1989 to 1992. Through reading, teaching, and engaging in discussions with other women, I had come to realise that the formal liberation of women in China since 1949 had been achieved at the cost of women's self-awareness, for very little attention had been given to transforming and reconstructing women's (or men's) self-understanding or values. As a result, a very traditional idea of gender roles and the division of labour continued to exist, though in variant forms. Equality between men and women effectively meant that women should take men as our models in every way. This had brought about considerable social progress, but such an idea of equality also had obvious disadvantages. First, physical differences between the sexes were ignored. Women were required to undertake heavy manual labour. When some women who had taken part in productive labour during the 1950s and 1960s were asked, "When did you become conscious of yourself as a woman?", they answered that it was after starting work, for in doing physical labour, they found that there were actual differences in physical strength between men and women (Min, 1997). Second, the tendency towards masculinising women went to extremes in terms of imitating men's behaviour, language, and clothing. For example, fashionable clothes became something unusual throughout China during the Cultural Revolution, when Chinese people were described as a 'blue sea' or 'green sea' from the colour of the uniform that both sexes wore at that time.

This growing awareness of 'becoming women' made some women begin to notice that "even though society initiated liberation and equality, women still remain as 'the second sex', as second class citizens" (Dai, 1999: 146). Another idea gained from de Beauvoir was relevant in this regard, namely, that the relationship between the women's movement and the proletarian revolution involved differences as well as connections – although here, too, I suspect that the influence of de Beauvoir's ideas occurred mainly retrospectively, and was used by scholars post hoc to explain social changes that had occurred autonomously.

What slowly came into existence was the broad conviction that although politics and economics are important, women's liberation also requires the transformation of gender, the transformation of the way being a woman or a man is understood, along with traditions and customs, and this process may turn out to be much harder than economic reform (see Li, X., 1988; Rong, 1994; Min, 1997).

A decade after *The Second Sex* was published in China, one of the criticisms of Li Xiaojiang's readings of de Beauvoir was that

> she does not consider Simone de Beauvoir to be her precursor; she does not discuss the status of Chinese women or Chinese feminism in relation to Simone de Beauvoir; she is not concerned with a fundamental or ontological gap between her own context and that of post-war France. This claim to *European* Enlightenment is linked equally to a belief in the legitimacy and primacy of the *Chinese* legacy of thinking about women's liberation *for Chinese women*. The grounds for this certainty in Li's thought is less cultural specificity than the organic, scientific, corporeal body that, in her view, all women share.
>
> (Barlow, 1997: 513–514)

In conversations I had with Li after reading Barlow and other articles on Chinese women's studies, Li seemed eager to clarify her point of view on Western feminism. She insisted:

> De Beauvoir's *The Second Sex* has not been given much importance in China, because her dynamic analysis of women was not as good as Marxism. The legacy of the theory of women that we accepted comes from Marxism. It is wiser, deeper and sharper than de Beauvoir's *The Second Sex*. Betty Friedan wrote *The Feminine Mystique* at the beginning of the 1960s, and she wanted women to get out of their family. If there had been the same sort of historical situation for Chinese women, this book would have created quite a stir in China. But the experiences of Chinese women were opposed to (American women). From the 1950s to the 1960s, especially during the Cultural Revolution, Chinese women were exhausted by working in society; how could you talk about 'the problem that has no name' to them? It is not to say because these books came from the West that we don't accept them. Exactly the reverse, it is due to our life experiences being so different.
>
> (interview, Min/Li, X., 3/3/1999)

Perhaps in response to Barlow's article, Li published articles reviewing Simone de Beauvoir's *The Second Sex* and Betty Friedan's *The Feminine Mystique* in 1999 and 2000, respectively. In her 1999 article, Li starts from her own experience of reading *The Second Sex*:

> To me, in reading this book, the important thing is the author's female standpoint of research on women and her attitude of self-reflexivity. It leads me to believe that wherever we live in this world, women do not live in solitude. We can start from ourselves to obtain knowledge of other women.
> (Li, X., 1999a: 99)

There are two reasons why Li disagrees with de Beauvoir's axiom that "one is not born, but rather becomes, a woman". One is that Li stresses that there are physical differences between women and men; the other is that a woman is indeed born, even though her 'second-sex' position is acquired as a product of male-centred societies. Li's insistence on what she sees as an ideologically and scientifically correct appreciation of the centrality of the material body is the starting point for her theory of sexual difference. This point will be discussed in more detail in the next part of this chapter.

It is apparent, even from this cursory examination of how *The Second Sex* travelled to and then within China, that the intellectual history involved is far more ambiguous than has been assumed. It has commonly been accepted that *The Second Sex* is the bible of the Western women's movement, and that de Beauvoir's book, along with *The Feminine Mystique*, are the key feminist classics (see Zhang, Y., 1991). In consequence, their real influence in China has not been examined. A number of interviews I conducted revealed that the reality was far more complex. Even though these two classic feminist books had travelled to China by the 1980s, they did not travel well inside China, where the political, economic, and cultural background was very different from that in the West. However, they did have an impact in women's studies circles and enlightened a number of pioneers of Chinese feminism in various ways.

Perhaps we need to look at not just one but several travelling stories of *The Second Sex*. Rosi Braidotti has expressed the opinion that although *The Second Sex* was published in France in 1949, it was not until the mid-1960s and the second wave of feminism in the United States that the book became an American political event. She writes:

> One could argue that intellectual history is full of such twists of fate and that the transmission of ideas, especially of politically revolutionary ones, is always made of such leaps, loops, and gaps.... Nevertheless, from a women's studies perspective, the point needs to be stressed; international dispersion and dissemination are forms of resistance, a way of preserving ideas which

may otherwise have been forgotten or destroyed, condemned to amnesia or to wilful obliteration, in their original contexts. Ideas, after all, are as mortal as their makers.

(Braidotti, 2000: 15–16)

Theorising the theory of women

> This new consciousness of identity self-described as an awakening, has under-gone an intellectual operation of a series of 'separations'. That is, theoretically, separate women's liberation from the 'proletarian emancipation' or the 'socialist revolution'; academically separate women's studies from traditional knowledge production of the humanities and social sciences; and strategically separate the women's movements from state moulding and control. Central to the project is to make 'women' a distinct category vis-a-vis the concept of 'class', and hence considering women's liberation to possess some meanings and goals which are different from or beyond those of class liberation and elimination.
>
> (Lin, Liu, and Jin, 1998: 112)

In the process of developing this theorising, the first task faced was that of deconstructing the traditional Marxist theory of women, which held that (1) women are a revolutionary force, (2) women's liberation is a condition of proletarian revolution, and (3) productive labour is the basic condition of women's liberation and is in itself progressive (see Barlow, 1994: 345). This theory had originally taken shape during the years of civil war in the 1920s and 1930s, and it is hard to deny that Chinese women did achieve extensive social liberation, as this ideology found expression in legislation and daily life. However, like all other areas of the party's rhetoric, it was challenged during the period of reform after 1978, as women turned out not to possess an unchanging essence, and thus many of the assumptions and ideas underlying the previous policies were shown to be false.

Even though Marxism continued to be the dominant tradition in China during the 1980s and early 1990s, the Women's Federation did shift its theoretical position, albeit in a rather ambiguous fashion. Marxist scholars in China commonly took production to be the primary material basis of women's liberation. The assumption that there is a positive correlation between economic growth and the advancement of women was accepted with little critical examination. As a consequence, the central task of the women's movement, as argued by some leading theorists, was considered to be developing social production and seeking liberation. Even those who acknowledged that material and technological progress would not automatically liberate women did not doubt that the ultimate remedy against the subordination of women lay in economic modernisation (Lin, Lui, and Jin, 1998). However, drawing on the new women's liberation theories, some criticism was voiced from inside the Women's Federation itself. Gao Xiaoxian, the director of the Shangxi Research Association for Women and Family in Shaanxi Province, was one such voice. In the 1980s, Gao remarked:

> At that time some scholars and the ACWF emphasised that, according to traditional Marxist theories, women's problems were due to low productive forces. In 1986, a lecture by Susan Green (an American scholar) led me to think that the development of productive forces is not the same as women's development. Then I wrote an article on modernisation and women's development, in which I argued that the modernisation of a society did not mean that women's problems would be sorted out automatically. . . . Indeed, because of the impact of Western theories on me at that time I could see the negative side of the market economy for women.
> (interview, Min/Gao, 14/7/1999)

However, not many scholars and activists of women's studies understood the problem for women that Gao had recognised, although we witnessed the defeat of women in the newly developing market economy. As support waned for the orthodox Marxist position of treating the women's question entirely under the heading of class, the ACWF was unable to challenge the current reform policy and had to shift its focus. Self-improvement rather than equality became the baseline of ACWF policy, and the problem identified was the 'low quality' (*suzhi di*) of women's lives. It was at its fifth congress in 1983 that the ACWF adopted the slogan of women's "Four Selves" (*Si zi*) – self-respect, self-love, self-possession, and self-improvement. And at its sixth congress in 1989, the Four Selves were changed to self-respect, self-reliance, self-confidence, and self-improvement. Out of this sixth congress came proposals that instead of relying on the protection of society and government, in a market economy women had to become more independent and rely only on themselves. Where did the idea of Four Selves come from? Jin Yihong, a feminist researcher in the Academy of Social Science in Jiangsu province, who has been involved in many co-operative projects with the Women's Federation in the province, pointed out:

> When Western feminism flows to China, it must find a meeting point. So far, the Women's Federation has accepted a great deal of feminist ideas, and the liberal feminist idea is the easiest to accept. Ideas such as 'reform', 'self-consciousness' and 'raising women's quality', all of these ideas which the ACWF has been developing since the 1980s have been influenced by this liberalism. Liu Bohong thinks that we are closer to socialist feminism.

I don't think so.... I think you cannot divide theory of women into different schools. However, Marxist theory of women is still the mainstream at the Women's Federation.

(interview, Min/Jin, 15/7/1999)

With the economic reforms intensifying in China in the late 1980s, it is no surprise that the liberal idea of Four Selves and self-improvement emerged in the discourse of the Women's Federation. This coincided with the government's dismantling of the welfare system which had sought to promote equality between men and women. Yet, it would be incorrect to assume that the Four Selves and self-improvement entirely replaced the traditional Marxist theory of women during this period of transformation.

During the second half of the 1980s, women's studies scholars confronted the fact that the theoretical world in China excluded theory of women, as women had not engaged with the mainstreaming of theory. Therefore, theorising and developing theory about women became an urgent challenge for the human sciences, which also had to contend with the political process of women's liberation. On this, Li Xiaojiang asserted:

> What is theory about women? Plainly put, theory about women consists of the abstractions made about women in philosophy. In practice, research on women confronts two different objects, each forming its own relatively independent theoretical category. So far as women's liberation is concerned, practice itself constitutes the first concrete object of theoretical research on women.
>
> (Li, X., 1988: 19–20)

For Li, forming abstractions on women through scientific methods was the scientific way of theorising women, and the 'new knowledge' would be the product of this process. The process of theorising women for Li should start from a process of 'separation':

> Women and class are two different categories: the former is human ontological and the latter, social historical. The making and evolution of the female sex was prior to the formation of classes and intrinsically transcends class relations.
>
> (Lin, Liu, and Jin, 1998: 113)

This is an early theoretical position, and it is understandable that emphasising the gendered identity of women was seen as a necessary development, given the long-standing overemphasis on class struggle by the Communist Party. Putting women into a category separate from class does, however, leave women's studies with the theoretical problem of theorising women.

Following this line, the initial theorising of theory had to concern itself with the question of 'sexual differences'. The discourse of 'nature' had been introduced, as noted earlier, by the writer Dia Qing. She emphasised the importance of distinguishing between males and females because "nature is set this way already. People do not have the power to change it" (Wang, Z., 1993: 205). In the same set of interviews, Wang Anyi commented:

> I think things move in waves. We are riding a brand new wave now. For example, now we have cosmetics. If you were to say that women shouldn't wear make-up and should be the same as men that just wouldn't do now. They should let us Chinese have this period of recognising sexual differences, let women enjoy their cosmetics. Later we may abandon such things.
> (Wang, Z., 1993: 166)

Although some scholars from abroad asserted that there is a danger in essentialising sexual differences (Barlow, 1994: 348), the response of some Chinese feminists was that

> the road of Chinese women's liberation is different from that of Western women's liberation because Chinese women have a different reality and past. For her, the 'equality of men and women' was once a mythical trap, and 'equal pay for equal work' was all but forced upon her. Gender difference is not a concept to be discarded or abandoned, but a necessary path through which she must pass.
> (Meng and Dai, 1989: 268–269)

Why had the theory of sexual difference in general been welcomed by scholars of women's studies in China? What Li Xiaojiang and many other women's studies scholars perceived as oppressive in the late 1980s and at the start of the 1990s was not that women had been made to symbolise the bodily sexual difference, but rather that a political or ideological discourse had rendered women invisible, suppressed their gender, and denied their difference from men. For them, the important task at hand was to awaken an awareness of gender identity among women by claiming the bodily differences and the physiological and psychological experiences that are particular to women.

Consequently, theorising *nuxing* (female gender) became the second important stage in undermining the old theory of women, a stage in which Li Xiaojiang was herself a leading figure. Any theorising of *nuxing* had to show that it represented women's lives as they really were, and it also had to reveal the grounding of its knowledge claims. Li Xiaojiang's influential book, *Eve's*

Exploration (1988), was the first work in which she problematised the concept of *nuxing*. In this work Li argued that, although physiology is not unimportant, it should not be treated as an *a posteriori* grounding for a theory of women's inequalities if it is to be in any way useful for activists and scholars. She also pointed out that the category of 'women' needs to be produced from the apparently non-gendered category of 'human being'. Overall, her argument is that

> the responsibility of the women's movement has always been to face women's reality and concretely measure and strategise ways of pushing women's liberation forward, but theory about women makes women in the abstract its foundation and it grasps the intrinsic qualities of the women's movement by connecting 'women as a category' on a conceptual level to other social categories.
>
> (Li, 1988: 21–22)

Li therefore concluded that Chinese women must take possession of the category 'women' and inscribe their own subjectivity within its framework.

In order to render woman the truly liberated subject, Li started her 'searching for self' journey by writing an autobiographical article "My Path to Womanhood", in which she shows how making oneself a subject offers a powerful way of theorising *nuxing*. In this essay, Li describes herself as a girl who excelled in a meritocratic world because she possessed a wholly androgynous will and could expend enormous efforts in pursuit of her goals. Li grew up in the world of 'equality', she never suffered any obvious sexual discrimination, and she was even appointed professor – and all of this without ever having to consider herself a woman. Motherhood opened her eyes, because she was suddenly confronted with the 'typical women's fate' in China: selfless domestic sacrifice made on top of the burden of her paid work. She felt that she was forced to play two roles at the same time and thus had to carry twice the load usually carried by a man. In this process she came to realise that

> the dual role women are obliged to play in everyday life entails dual philosophies of life. Such a duality splits a woman as a social entity and deprives her of the capacity to present herself as the perfect 'ego' in both family and social life. But the question baffles me: why are women alone made to suffer in this manner?
>
> (Li, X., 1994b: 105)

Though it was her personal story, Li Xiaojiang used it to reveal the vanishing of women's personal lives and thus question the traditional official gender theory and practices.[5]

Rereading Li's writings after 20 years and rethinking the process of theorising *nuxing* in the 1980s raises two issues. First, the process of theorising *nuxing* positioned women as gendered and foundational subjects, considered to be the 'real' life of women. But how could their personal lives be linked with the big picture of the party, the state, and society, while leaving us the space to think freely about the problem? And second, if *nuxing* was the real subjected position of women, then what could there be that was new in theorising about women? If the old Marxist theory left no room to recognise the personal, then how could 'women' be understood to refer to individuals? It seems that Li wrote her life story precisely in order to make the theory of *nuxing* intelligible at the ground level and as a self-reflective social reality. Together with many of her generation, Li wanted to promote a human subject independent of the party and traditional culture and see it as the model of a liberated subject. However, as Feng Xu noted, "It could be said that they both fell into the same trap of voluntarism from a new direction: the equation of an independent human individual subject with an emancipated subject" (Xu, 2009: 204–205).

As elsewhere, theorising theory in China has been largely shaped by the socio-political context. Unfortunately, the process of theorising *nuxing* had to cease abruptly in 1989. The reason behind this was that although women's studies as a discipline continued to develop after 1989, the changing political climate in China presented enormous problems for intellectual development; after the events of Tiananmen Square in particular, great care had to be taken in theorising theory. Without freedom of thought, reconceptualising the world and using a new conceptual language were difficult if not impossible tasks, and the lack of resources and funding imposed serious material constraints. Up until the middle of the 1990s, attracting funding from outside China for research came to be seen as the only way to ease the financial problems experienced by most centres for women's studies, but unless research projects were oriented towards practical policies and were expressed in current (that is, US-dominated) conceptual terms, it was very difficult to attract financial support from international sources or, for that matter, from private donors. In this context, theorising about even such fundamental notions as sexual difference and *nuxing* had to take a back seat.

The process involved in travelling feminism that I have outlined here is unlike the development of theory in women's studies in the West, which was based on a distinct feminist movement and its associated claims for equality between men and women. Theorising theory by the Women's Federation and women's studies scholars in China was not the result of a feminist movement. Its development began with women starting to meditate upon the equality that Chinese women had supposedly achieved from 1949, while at the same time debating the relationship between what they knew about Western feminism and their experience of traditional Marxist theory of women. Theorising theory at this stage reflected a more general trend towards liberalism in Chinese social theory. Modernisation was seen in liberal terms as economic development without interference from the state, and the market economy of Western, developed nations was viewed as the model for modernisation. This liberal approach was typical of the official line of the ACWF and of women's studies scholars in academic circles.

Afterthoughts

The social, political, and economic background of women's studies in China differs considerably from that in Western countries. One of the important factors is that gender equality gave way to gender difference during the process of economic reform launched in the late 1970s. The result was that

> Chinese feminism today may be caught up in a historical juncture that requires *reconstructing* binary gender, rather than a *deconstruction* of gender, as advocated at this historical moment in a West where modern sexual differentiation and gender identity have well-established and hegemonic histories.
>
> (Yang, 1999: 36)

However, the reinvention of the Chinese Enlightenment might appear in retrospect to be a very particular moment in the history of thinking about the Chinese women's movement, and at this moment the metaphor of awakening was used once again to imply that instead of overvaluing Western conceptual tools, Chinese women's collective consciousness should be raised from the gender unconsciousness that characterised Chinese society.

Most of the feminist ideas that travelled to China during the 1980s came from the Western feminist movement of the 1960s, 1970s, and 1980s. Of the different strands of feminism, liberal feminism proved the most successful, and the term 'choice' came to play an important role – as it did in neoliberal feminism in the United States during the 1980s. "Since the concept of choice is essential to participation in democracy, it also had an emphasis towards consumer culture. Feminism was engaged in a struggle with neoliberalism but also dependent on it for its existence" (Grewal, 2005: 28). However, in China we failed to grasp the American understanding and use of the term choice. When translated into the Chinese language, the academic concept of choice tended to be associated with the trend of liberal thought of the postsocialist context. It was during this time that Chinese women's studies scholars played an important role in translating Western second-wave feminist ideas (asserting gender justice within state-organised capitalism) into Chinese ideas (asserting gender justice or gender difference within state-organised socialism).

However, as we have seen, certainly after 1949, several ideas did not travel as well as others. The theory of 'socialist feminism' which was developed during the period of second-wave feminism did not travel at all well. After experiencing the hard life associated with the extreme left of the Cultural Revolution, any word related to the term 'left' or 'socialism' was decidedly unwelcome. The thoughts developed in the West during the 1980s on 'women and development' and 'gender and development' did not travel to China until the 1990s. Perhaps this was due to the fact that the discourse of modernisation was dominant in mainstream thinking, and according to the prevalent understanding of modernisation, development concerned 'backward' Third World countries. Chinese academics and researchers felt little inclination to engage with these countries, as their own society was steeped in the discourse of modernisation. They envisioned and recognised that the relationship between modernisation and the capitalist market economy needs people to be experienced with and connected to a fully developed market economy.[6]

From the beginning of the 1980s, women's studies and feminist ideas travelled to China into those few spaces in intellectual and political life which were no longer occupied by the state and its ideologies. In academic circles, these ideas first had an impact on scholars in foreign literature and language studies, following which they travelled to other subjects. The ideas mainly influenced those researchers who were already familiar with aspects of Western literature or history, while other scholars took much less notice. During this initial stage, the ideas travelled in specific and focused ways which depended very much on personal contacts, existing knowledge, ability to engage with English-language publications, and pre-dispositions derived from prior intellectual concerns. In the 1980s, the term feminism was still a taboo in the official Chinese women's organisation, the ACWF, and ideas associated with it did not travel far at all. (This issue will be discussed at length in Chapter 3.) However, the subject of women's studies, as a new way to discuss women's problems, was adopted by the ACWF in their state feminist framework during the 1980s, and this provided a route by which the Sinicization of these and associated ideas could take place. The work of Li Xiaojiang and other scholars provides an interesting case study of how thinking through these things – and gradually moving from a conventional 'Marxist theory of women' position to a reworking of the Western concept of sexual difference as the Sinicized *nuxing* – took place, and also of how this later enabled rethinking the form of theory as much as its content.

In retrospect, the awakening of Chinese women in the 1980s was, I think, not so much a radical break with what existed before as it was the development of a network of complex continuities and discontinuities. Using the term 'awakening', which comes from the May Fourth Movement, to characterise this process would imply that what China needs is another enlightenment – and perhaps also that the tools of the West are required to question and reconceptualise Chinese culture and Marxist theory of women. This would be to discount the legacy of socialist feminism and the important gains it secured for Chinese women.

Indeed, the wave of Chinese women's studies and feminism in the 1990s was quite different from that of the 1980s. Where Chinese women's studies in the 1980s was dominated by Chinese scholars and activists, contemporary global trends became much more noticeable in the 1990s. Although Marxist theory of women remained the official line of thought in the Women's Federation, the trend of asserting the global and transnational feminist ideas became a new wave in academic women's studies circles and the Women's Federation. This new trend in China towards the global and towards transnational feminism was to interrupt the newly developed Chinese women's and gender studies. What the Chinese women's movement needed on the brink of the 1990s was dialogue with contemporary transnational feminism.

Notes

1 A number of studies on this issue have been published since 2000. For example, Barlow (2004); Ko and Wang (2007); and Judge (2008).
2 The ACWF was set up in 1949 as the mass organisation designated to mobilise and represent Chinese women. Since there was no government department in China in charge of women's affairs, the ACWF was granted the authority and resources to help interpret and implement state policies regarding women. The ACWF was established to act as a bridge, a two-way channel of communication between women and established branches throughout the country (Zhang with Xu, 1995). By 1994, it laid claim to 68,355 branches: 30 at the provincial level, 370 at city level, 2,810 at county level and 65,145 at township level, totalling 80,000–90,000 cadres (Howell, 1996).
3 For more detail on this, see Tan (1992); Barlow (1994); Li, X. (1994a); Lin, C. (1997); and Min (1999).
4 Previously known as the College for the Training of Women Administrative Cadres, run by the ACWF during the 1980s.
5 Perhaps among the factors that led Li Xiaojiang to pay such close attention to Chinese women's personal lives were her personal conversations in 1988 with women soldiers who had fought in the war against Japan. Their stories taught her to be aware of the theoretical importance of female individuals and local matters. In order to study the hidden history of Chinese women, and inspired by the method of oral history from abroad, Li began her comprehensive project in 1992: "Oral History of Chinese Women in the 20th Century". The project ran to four volumes, which were published in 2003 by Sanlian Publishing House in Beijing. See Li, Xiaojiang (2013), "Responding to Tani Barlow: Women's Studies in the 1980s", *Differences*, 24 (2), pp. 172–181.
6 One of the statements on this issue came from abroad. See Wang, Lingzhen (2013), "Gender and Sexual Differences in 1980s China: Introducing Li Xiaojiang", *Differences*, 24 (2), pp. 8–21.

3 *Duihua* (dialogue) in-between

The process of translating the terms 'feminism' and 'gender' in China

> Feminists and activists in global activism must also begin to address the language barriers that are evident in current international feminist dialogue. It is essential not only to pay attention to spoken words that have different meanings, but, even more important, to recognise the cultural and ideological paradigms which underlie language differences.
>
> (Hsiung and Wong, 1998: 491)

In 1992, a conference on "Engendering China: Women, Culture and the State" was hosted by Harvard University and Wellesley College in the United States. Its organisation and content were typical of the initial dialogue between women's studies scholars from China and the West (mostly from the United States). Sharon K. Hom, an American-Chinese law professor, later recalled her experience of this conference:

> As I sat listening to the presentation in English, invoking terms such as 'strategic subject positionalities', and 'counter-hegemonic reification', I wondered how Chinese translators were dealing with these terms that even many English-speaking listeners would find mystifying. This was a moment of recognition of cross-cultural and linguistic 'cross-talk' that often goes unnoticed and unremarked upon, especially in international and comparative legal work.
>
> (Hom, 1997: 1)

Laurel Bossen, a Canadian professor, also noticed that the biggest issue at the conference was that of translation: there were so many terms she found difficult to comprehend. As communication between Chinese and Western scholars was hampered by the language barrier, Bossen suggested that before holding this kind of conference again, a dictionary of all the important terms should be produced, such as feminism, women, female, and so forth (as reported in Li, X., 2000a). Interestingly, these questions of translation were not addressed by most of the delegates from mainland China, perhaps because this was the first time they had any communication with their Western counterparts. Or, more likely, since most delegates from mainland China did not understand the English language, the issue of translation was not important for them. According to some of the Chinese delegates, owing to the lack of a 'common' language in which to communicate, many of the Western scholars remained silent on the matters that the Chinese scholars were speaking about. In fact, the main dialogue or argument about feminism occurred primarily between the Chinese scholars and students from mainland China who were studying in the United States (Du, 1997, and particularly Li, X., 2000a). The news about this first contact from the 'contact zone' was exciting, but it was also revealed that great communicative complications existed between feminists from the West, from mainland China, and from yet other nations.

Following this event, one concern was how to address the issue of translation. With the transnational feminisms intensifying as they travelled through China in the 1990s, issues of translation started emerging in Chinese women's studies circles. Perhaps as a result of dealing with such issues in everyday life and being involved in translation projects, most of the concern came from overseas Chinese women's studies scholars (Hom, 1997; Lin, C., 1997; Wang, Z., 1997a; Hsiung and Wong, 1998; Min, 2007, 2008). From their domestic counterparts, apart from a few articles addressing some issues of translation following the Fourth World Conference on Women (FWCW) in Beijing in 1995 (Feng, 1996; Qi, 1997; Li, X., 1999b, 2002), there was silence.

Generally, anxiety about translation issues began with looking for the right words, noticing language barriers in current international feminist dialogue, and asking how to negotiate the shaping of meaning by political and cultural forces. My own interest concerns the matter of what it is that we should be anxious or concerned about when doing translation. Is translation just a matter of looking for the right words, or is there something going on beyond the words themselves? And if so, what precisely is this? What else do we know or can we say about translation and its implications for cross-cultural understanding? And indeed, what does it mean for a feminist scholar to cross the language barrier between two or more cultures and linguistic communities?

With these ideas in mind, I will examine the processes of translating the terms feminism and gender, two of the concepts crucial to the travelling theory of women's and gender studies and from which the terms arose, circulated, and acquired legitimacy in China in the 1980s and 1990s. However, my focus is not on translation in the ordinary sense of the word, much less its technical aspects. I regard translation as a process of dialogue and negotiation, which is entered into by the translators; so, using *duihua* (dialogue) as a metaphor, I will discuss certain aspects of this process of *duihua* and negotiation between the different languages and cultures on the part of different translators. Here, by 'in-between', I refer to that "space of translation where the self or one culture encounters, and, more importantly, *interacts* with an 'other' or another culture" (Dingwaney, 1995: 8). In this space, the dominant language and culture is interpreted, rewritten, inflected, or subverted by the native speakers in their own accents.

In taking a closer look at this we have to ask, who is the translator? Is it the in-between? As the focus of my investigation, I have chosen three key translators which came into existence at different times and in different parts of China. These are the All-China Women's Federation (ACWF), based in Beijing; the Chinese women's studies scholars and activists, based throughout mainland China; and the Chinese Society for Women's Studies (CSWS), based in the United States but operating largely through email-based discussion and including diverse opinions and viewpoints from other parts of the world. To demonstrate the different meanings that each translator activated in the process of their translation, I hope not only to show how they gave new life to the originals that they translated, but also to see how they identified the kind of life they discerned in the originals, and how they aimed to inject this into the target language version for a particular time and a particular readership. This process, of course, also involves a power relationship.

Translating 'feminism'

Feminism in the 1980s: a forbidden word and breaking the taboo

The term feminism has a century-long history in China. It was translated into Chinese at the turn of the twentieth century, when it entered China along with the suffrage movement. The original translation was *nuquan zhuyi* (women's power or rights + ism), which denotes militant demands for women's political rights, reminiscent of the earlier women's suffrage movements in the West and in China.[1] After the decline of the feminist movement in China, the women's movement took another and very different direction, that of advancing the development of women's liberation through the socialist political struggle. Thus, the identity of Chinese women was defined by the ACWF and other state organisations exclusively in terms of an official discourse on gender. The use of the term feminism has been rejected – 'forbidden' – within this discourse since 1949.

When feminist knowledge travelled to China during the 1980s, the key term feminism emerged in Chinese women's studies discourse again. The new translation proposed in the 1990s was *nuxing zhuyi* (femininity + ism), which in fact emphasises gender differences rather than women's rights and is seen in China to denote a far richer cultural and political meaning than the earlier term. This term has been in circulation for the past decades in Hong Kong and Taiwan and became widely accepted in mainland China in the 1990s.

Although some scholars think that the Chinese Communist Revolution was intrinsically feminist (Lin, C., 1997; Yang, 1999), the state-sponsored women's organisation, the ACWF, has been very careful to distinguish its Marxist theory of women from the 'bourgeois feminism' of the West. However, when women's studies emerged in China from the middle of the 1980s on, the term feminism also came into the language through translated Western documents (Wan, 1988), and the original 'political' translation – *nuquan zhuyi* – has been used since then. Women's studies scholars at that time were breaking a taboo with regard to feminism by bringing not only feminist questions into women's studies via Marxist history, but also the term and the political ideas. This process was started by Chinese women's studies scholars, among them Li Xiaojiang, who argued in Marxist terms that history has produced three stages of theorising about women – one of which is 'bourgeois feminist theory' – a stage that included the Paris Commune and the middle-class feminist rights movement. She also emphasised that a great many changes had occurred in Western feminism since the 1960s, and that if Chinese scholars failed to study these new developments and continued to dismiss them as bourgeois feminism, it would make it impossible for China to participate in international theoretical debates (Li, X., 1988).

At this point in her work, Li Xiaojiang borrowed the Western term feminism as a way of challenging the Communist Party's Marxist theory of women and questioning the legitimacy of the ACWF. Consequently, her work was criticised as itself being bourgeois feminism by the ACWF's old guard. For the ACWF, the term feminism was obviously part of a bourgeois ideology and thus against the principles of 'correct' Marxism. However, like most of the party's rhetoric, the old Marxist theory of women was being challenged during the period of reform because it failed to represent the reality of women's lives and current ideas about how to theorise these. As such, it was out of date, not to mention politically and intellectually discredited. Therefore, the ACWF's counter-accusation that Li engaged in bourgeois feminism was ineffectual, and failed to receive support among academic scholars and among some of the younger members of the ACWF (Wang, Z., 1997a).

In general, however, the attitude of the younger generation of the ACWF cadres and some women's studies scholars towards feminism was still hesitant. For instance, Liu Bohong, the vice director of the Institute of Women's Studies in the ACWF, commented: "I maintained a sharp vigilance about feminism during the 1980s, because feminism was negated by Marxism. I never thought about introducing feminism to Chinese women at that time" (interview, Min/Liu, 4/3/1999). Worrying about political control was another problem. One women's studies scholar told me:

> The first time I heard the word feminism was in 1985. At that time I felt so confused and worried about it. Talking feminism in China would

involve two forbidden domains which were the Party-State and men. You can't criticise the Party and the government, because being against the Party means against men, and most leaders of the Party and the government are men!

(interview, Min/Du, 7/4/1999)

With the relaxation of political control, the taboos surrounding bourgeois feminism gradually broke down, and the term *nuquan zhuyi* began to appear quite frequently in women's studies publications from the middle of the 1980s – in most cases, though, only in translations of Western feminist writings. There was some research conducted on feminism, but only seldom did Chinese women call themselves feminists. Why was that? On this subject, Li Xiaojiang has commented:

> It is interesting to note that the term *feminism* is seldom used to describe women's activities in China, whether governmental or nongovernmental, academic or general. . . . For the Women's Federation, the term *feminism* is obviously seen as part of a bourgeois ideology and thus against the principles of Marxism. For scholars in unofficial women's studies groups, however, avoiding the term *feminism* or not identifying their work as 'feminist' is a deliberate and voluntary choice rather than a political consideration. Such scholars respect Western-based feminist theory, and yet they still believe that Chinese Women's Studies has its own background and circumstances unique to Chinese history and social reality.
>
> (Li and Zhang, 1994: 148)

Although Li was one of the pioneers of women's studies in China during the 1980s, she also kept her distance from Western feminism. Indeed, as Li pointed out, avoiding the term feminism was a deliberate choice, because at that time we believed that China was a socialist country and that women's problems could be solved in a different manner.

This seems to accurately represent the attitude of other women's studies scholars towards feminism in the late 1980s. A famous example of this is provided by the article "Three Interviews: Wang Anyi, Zhu Lin, Dai Qing". In this article, three leading contemporary women writers from mainland China all rejected the label of 'feminist', with Wang Anyi's response also representing the views of the other two:

> In China women are only now beginning to have the right, the luxury to talk about the differences between men and women, to enjoy something that distinguishes women from men. That is the reason I absolutely deny that I am a feminist.
>
> (Wang, Z., 1993: 165)

These three writers understood feminism in the West as denying any distinction between men and women, and this they thought unacceptable, emphasising instead a 'natural' harmony between the sexes: "Nature is set this way already. People do not have the power to change it, so we should treat it with awe and try to maintain harmony" (Wang, Z., 1993: 205). Sheng Ying, a women's literary critic, adopted a similar approach:

> I think women have some masculinity and men have some femininity. They have mutual benefit. I gained this idea from Virginia Woolf's 'androgyny'. It is easy to accept this idea in Chinese culture. I think gender as understood in Chinese society is evidently opposed to understand in Western societies. We emphasise harmony between the two sexes in oriental societies.
> (interview, Min/Sheng, 17/2/1999)

This point of view was representative of a good many Chinese women, and it rejected what was seen as the denial of women's 'female nature' through such a long period of 'masculinising the feminine' between the 1950s and the 1970s.

Most Chinese women's studies scholars and women writers of that time took care to avoid the label feminist, even as they published sophisticated views on the politics of gender, and even though those views may very well be regarded as feminist by scholars from the West. For instance, in the 1980s, the names of Virginia Woolf, Simone de Beauvoir, and a number of other Western feminists were frequently mentioned and referred to in a favourable way in the writings of female Chinese thinkers who nonetheless refused to call themselves feminists.

In order to understand this complex situation, one must take into account Chinese women's relationship with the state, and with official feminism through its representative, the ACWF. In the 1980s, the ACWF still took a strong position on all gender issues, claiming to represent women and to protect their rights, but in reality operating very much like other hegemonic organisations controlled by the party, even though it was the least important of all the Chinese state bodies.

The approach of women in academia was both similar to and different from what Barlow describes. Chinese women's studies scholars, myself among them, were not very much concerned about how to translate the term feminism, but we were concerned about our position in relation to what we assumed this term to entail. For instance, in my women's studies classes in the 1980s, I introduced a spectrum of feminist thought, from liberal to radical, but as for how these related to our lives, our society, I couldn't say with certainty. Sun Xiaomei, who taught at the Women's Federation Cadres College, said to me: "Mainly, I introduced feminism in our class and my students were interested in it, but I didn't think feminism was useful for us, and the students had a similar feeling" (interview, Min/Sun, 9/3/1999).

Therefore, the problem that women's studies faced in China over the term feminism from the 1980s to the early 1990s was not "how do we translate it?"

but "should we use it or not?" From around the middle of the 1990s, a different approach to feminism developed in China, perhaps in response to the more open and inclusive approach of feminists across the world, as I shall discuss next.

Feminism in the 1990s: how should it be translated?

By the mid of 1990s, the new translation of feminism as *nuxing zhuyi* (femininity + ism) had replaced the old term *nuquan zhuyi* (women's rights + ism) in most places, and it is now widely used in contemporary women's studies writing. This new translation travelled from Taiwan and Hong Kong. In China, the new wave of 'transnational feminism' arrived with the idea of *jiegui* (connecting with the international track of thought) during the 1990s. As cultural exchanges increased rapidly with Taiwan and Hong Kong from the 1980s, many Western ideas were imported into China from these places. The term *nuxing zhuyi* and *nuquan zhuyi* were used as titles of conferences and workshops (Du, 1996), and a few Chinese women even called themselves feminists (Huang, W., 1995; Dai, 1999). Criticism of bourgeois feminism largely disappeared, although official Marxist theory of women kept its distance from the term feminism. It is important to note that both women's studies scholars and the new generation of the ACWF have accepted the new translation. In the context of changing attitudes to feminism, there is no sharp distinction between women scholars and women from the ACWF, although different opinions on the translation of the term feminism have emerged between women in China and Chinese women's studies scholars in the West. It seems that the initial problem people faced in China over the term feminism – "should it be used or not?" – had shifted to "how should it be translated?" How and why did this change occur, and what was the range of attitudes towards translation issues? What specific issues occurred with regard to the translation of this particular term? And why did the new translation *nuxing zhuyi* gradually replace the previously preferred translation?

When the new wave of transnational feminism arrived in China during the 1990s, the issue of translation was addressed in women's studies circles. An article by Li Xiaojiang saw the issues involved in the following way:

> As a friend explained it to me, the problem is not between Eastern and Western women, but is the problem of translation. Feminism should be translated into either 'men and women equality' or 'men and women equal power + ism', but not '*nuquan zhuyi*'. Actually, we all understand that once the concept is being used widely, it is very difficult to correct or change it, and seems unnecessary.
>
> (Li, X., 1995: 97)

This attitude towards translating the term feminism was at this time shared by a large number women's studies scholars in China, myself included. We believed that no matter how much attention was given to producing the 'correct' translation, readers would have their own understanding of the term, based on the particular cultural and intellectual context in which they found themselves.

Some Chinese women's studies scholars, however, took the translation issue in another direction. This time, it was more of an academic concern. Zhang Jingyuan, who studied feminist literature in the United States and returned to China at the end of the 1980s, edited a translation of *The Contemporary Feminist Critique* in 1992. In her introduction, she addressed the issue of translating the term feminism:

> There are two translations of the term of feminism in China, *nuquan zhuyi* and *nuxing zhuyi*. Obviously, the difference between them is *quan* (power or rights) and *xing* (sex). *Nuquan/nuxing zhuyi* is the theory that studies gender and power. Indeed, it would be wonderful if there were a Chinese word which can include the meaning of both gender and power. But there is not such a word, so we have to choose one of them (*nuquan/nuxing*).
>
> (Zhang, J., 1992: 4)

Zhang then traces the history of translating feminism into Chinese in the twentieth century, and divides this history into two periods associated with the Chinese women's movements. The early period of the women's movement focused on the fight for equal rights with men, so the appropriate translation was *nuquan zhuyi*. Although this movement had not finished, Zhang asserted:

> If we emphasise integrating the meaning of 'gender' into feminism, this means we are entering the period of post-structuralism of gender . . . in this book, we have included articles of a post-structuralist feminist kind, therefore using the term '*nuxing zhuyi*' is more appropriate. However, here the word '*xing*' (sex) implies the meaning of '*quan*' (power), or it is being empowered with new meaning.
>
> (Zhang, J., 1992: 4)

For Zhang, in using the term *nuxing zhuyi* as a translation for feminism, her concern was how to introduce more updated feminist ideas, particularly the theory of gender, to Chinese readers.

Dai Jinhua, a leading feminist scholar who has introduced various Western feminist theories into China since the 1980s, had similar ideas about translating the term feminism. She recalled the history of translating feminism into Chinese during the 1980s in the following way:

> For the issue of translation, generally speaking I believe that meaning is established by users. It is important to make the word easy to understand. . . . In 1988, when we discussed the translation issues about some basic

> concepts and terms of feminism, we have had no very clear idea about it. But we preferred to use the term *nuxing zhuyi* to translate the term feminism itself, because there was too much prejudice and misunderstanding of this word. We wanted to apply a new translation to produce a new meaning. At that time, men or women, in support or against feminism, all concentrated on the word 'power' when they thought of feminism and presumed that feminism is a social movement for protecting women's rights. No doubt this is a very important part of feminism, but nevertheless it is just a part. What concerned us more about feminism/*nuxing zhuyi* is focusing the term on women ourselves: the practices of different cultures between the genders, the different experiences of gender, and the organisation of gender in our social history. Therefore, we wanted very much to include the meaning of 'gender' in our translation.
>
> (Dai, 1999: 146–147)

Interestingly, for many people, *nuxing zhuyi* sounded 'softer' than *nuquan zhuyi*, although to Dai and her friends, translating feminism into *nuxing zhuyi* was a matter of strategy. But they were certainly also concerned about other things:

> During the 1980s, we advocated an elite specialist culture and agreed that we should resist the mainstream culture, one aspect of which was the official ideology that theory should serve for practice. Therefore, we emphasised very clearly that we were not 'practical' feminists, but scholars who studied gender in the sense of the academic and the cultural. A feminist intellectual – in fact, this is definitely my identity from that time to today.
>
> (Dai, 1999: 147–148)

Clearly, this strategy of translation indicates the use of the new translation of the term feminism. Zhang and Dai, two Chinese feminist scholars, tried to take the power of theorising women from the hands of mainstream academia and official ideology by 're-theorising' Chinese women.

Zhang Jingyuan and Dai Jinhua are among the Chinese scholars who are familiar with Western feminist theories. Their ideas about translation are clear, and by using the new *nuxing zhuyi* for the term feminism, they assign it a new meaning. Their negotiation between Western feminist theory and the political and cultural specificity of China has had a great impact on establishing feminism in China.

Zhang and Dai's ideas represented thinking about translating the term feminism in academic circles from the end of 1980s through the 1990s, but it is also important to consider what the 'practical' women's studies scholars and activists in China thought about translating the term. A significant event in this context was a discussion on the translation issue during a two-week workshop on "Chinese Women and Development" which took place at Tianjin Normal University in China in 1993. Regarding the term feminism, most participants agreed that *nuquan zhuyi* refers to Western women's struggle for equal rights with men, while *nuxing zhuyi* describes Chinese women's efforts to express their own desires and points of view, but with no connotation of a militant political movement. Participants argued that *nuquan zhuyi* requires women to follow men's standards (equality), while *nuxing zhuyi* builds up a female culture and uses women's points of view to remould society with men in it (difference). Most participants preferred using the translation *nuxing zhuyi* because it corresponded with the actual situation in China (Hom, 1993).

This discussion encapsulates the reasons for which the translation *nuquan zhuyi* was replaced with *nuxing zhuyi*. Having experienced endless political movements since 1949, most Chinese intellectual women wanted to distance themselves from overtly political discourse. A cultural turn had emerged in women's studies.

The new discourse of *nuxing* represented the rethinking of Marxist theory of women concerning how to re-engage with the subject of women. In addition, Chinese women's studies scholars and activists wanted to use the new translation *nuxing zhuyi* to empower women. This translation fitted the new discourse of *nuxing* (female) very well, and was more likely to be accepted by society. Furthermore, some Chinese women's studies scholars thought that the new interpretation not only fitted the context of China, but also widened the understanding of feminism in the West. As Hu Haili, another scholar of women's studies, explained, the changed interpretation of the term feminism from *nuquan zhuyi* to *nuxing zhuyi* reflected a distinct trend: the women's movement and women's studies in developed countries were no longer seen as just fighting for equal rights with men in order to advance women's interests; they were instead seen as devoted to changing the cultural mechanisms which produced gender inequality (Hu, personal letter, 24/7/1998). Although the 'culture craze' (*wenhua re*) of the 1980s had cooled down during the 1990s, the term culture still influenced the understanding the feminism.

However, in 1999, what I found during my fieldwork was that most of my interviewees preferred the translation *nuquan zhuyi* for the term feminism. However, some interviewees used both terms, *nuquan zhuyi* and *nuxing zhuyi*, in the interviews, perhaps indicating that the term that they used was not a particularly important issue for them. One of the reasons for this change might have been linked to the intensive transnational feminist exchange following the 1995 UN women's conference.[2]

Furthermore, it is worth noting that a new understanding of feminism has emerged in China, one which does not avoid the political issues, but instead asserts that feminists should be more involved in the promotion of democracy in China. As Li Huiying commented:

> The development of feminism should be linked with the process of democracy in China. If there is no promoting of the movement of democracy, there is no foundation for feminism.
>
> (interview, Min/Li, H., 3/3/1999)

When I talked with leading scholars of women's studies in 1999, I was informed that more political terms had been used to interpret the word feminism – individualism and subjectivity among them. As the sociologist Tan Shen related:

> There is a long tradition of individualism in America. Therefore, feminism was born from there. There is no tradition of individualism in China, so there is no soil for growing feminism. . . . Of course, the women's movement should reflect the subjectivity of women. Under this situation of lack of individual subjectivity, we should overcome it with men, and unite as much as possible with the groups of women who have been neglected in our society.
>
> (interview, Min/Tan, 8/3/1999)

However, what is Chinese women's studies and, in particular, what part in it should be played by circumstances and ideas unique to Chinese history and social reality? This question has been puzzling me and many other Chinese women's studies scholars since the 1980s. In 1999, after talking with pioneers of women's studies during my fieldwork, I found that this was very much a typical response:

> The dominant powers in history are patriarchy and men, but there is a difference between them. For example, there was patriarchy but not necessarily men's rights; certainly there was matriarchal power but no women's rights in Chinese history. It is a fact that in Western history there were neither women's rights nor matriarchal power. . . . Therefore, it is very important to join women's rights and human rights together in China, because they are both lacking in our society. However, in Western societies, they first established human rights, but this didn't include women, so feminists fought for the rights of women. In Chinese society, under circumstances without individual rights, the government offered women's rights. The liberation of Chinese women as a collective group exceeds individual rights, so we know there are many drawbacks, because the rights of the individual are important.
>
> (interview, Min/Li, X., 3/3/1999)

It is worth noting the links between feminism, individualism, women's rights, and human rights identified by Li. Those who took trips abroad most often to the United States during the 1990s often shifted their understanding of feminism in a political direction. However, liberal feminism still took the lead in the new trend of transnational feminism.

Was a different translation of the term feminism necessary in order to draw a line between the West and China? This question emerged when these two translations of feminism were circulated. Thus, when the translation *nuxing zhuyi* appeared in China, Li Xiaojiang argued that it should be a deliberate strategy to use *nuquan zhuyi* when referring to Western feminist thought, emphasising its political basis, but for feminism to be translated as *nuxing zhuyi* when referring to the Chinese experience, because this translation emphasises the cultural above the political (Li, X., 1995). The question remains: if the term feminism is divided between *nuquan zhuyi* and *nuxing zhuyi*, does this entail emphasising differences between women in China and women from abroad? The debate on the translation of feminism in the CSWS provides an interesting example.

Translation across borders: the case of translating 'feminism' in the CSWS

In order to introduce more Western feminism to Chinese women's studies, the CSWS, a 'new translator', emerged in the border area between China and the West during the 1990s.

Noting that some Chinese scholars did not call themselves feminists because they were not familiar with the term, members of CSWS suggested:

> We find there is ambivalence and a lack of clarity about feminism and women's studies in Western countries on the part of Chinese scholars. Thus, more studies about Western feminism need to be conducted, and more exchanges between scholars inside and outside China should be initiated.
> (Zhang with Xu, 1995: 37)

Following this mission, the CSWS organised several projects introducing Chinese scholars to feminism and women's studies in the West in the 1990s. In 1994 and 1997, the CSWS also organised a group to write and translate into Chinese two books about Western feminism and women's studies. During my membership of the CSWS, I was involved in these projects. As I have already mentioned, in every project there was much debate among CSWS members through letters and emails (the early days of information technology) on how to translate the term feminism, how to define the meaning of the term, and how to clarify for all those involved the contextual differences between doing women's studies in China and in the West. Here, I refer to an online discussion in 1997 as an example of how the CSWS saw the translation issues involved.[3]

Wang Zheng, one of the editors of the translation project, noted in a letter that some contributors emphasised that the English term feminism had very rich connotations, and therefore no one single translation or explanation in Chinese could do justice to such a complex phenomenon. Neither *nuquan zhuyi* nor *nuxing zhuyi* conveyed everything entailed by the term feminism, and therefore the historical background should be acknowledged when the term is translated (Wang, Z. letter to members of the CSWS, 1994). In other words, translation was seen as the process by which the correct words were found to match the original meaning. The discussion began with two themes:

Nuquan zhuyi – a political enterprise.
Nuxing zhuyi – an academic term or essentialism.

Taking exception to translating feminism as *nuxing zhuyi*, some contributors preferred the translation *nuquan zhuyi*. Considering feminism an engaged, political enterprise, they reasoned that this should be emphasised in the translation and found *nuxing zhuyi* inadequate for this purpose (see Wei, email, 30/4/1997). Other contributors, however, thought that *nuxing zhuyi* sounded more academic, and that this might be why it was used in Taiwan, because the feminist movement in Taiwan began in academia on the basis of imported feminist ideas (Chau, email, 30/4/1997).

A member of the group, Chau, reviewed a number of articles on feminist history and feminist dictionaries. From this, Chau commented that the problem was not defining feminism, but rather (literally) translating the word:

> Feminism is strange and unique to begin with in the West – I suggest someone look up the history of the word in a feminist thought dictionary. I suspect that like many 'isms' the word was first coined by someone who was against feminism and wanted to laugh at it by giving it a (at that time) ludicrous name: feminine and femininity are the very opposite ideas of feminism. So unless we want to assert a cultural feminist standpoint – arguing that because women are so different from men by nature we should have complementary social tasks though enjoying equal power/rights – we should avoid any term that suggests sex/gender essentialism.
> (Chau, email, 30/4/1997)

In the meantime, Wang discussed the origin of the term feminism with Karen Offen, a historian of European feminism. Offen's response to Wang was that "translating 'feminism' is always a concern – the best definition is something like 'a theory and practice aimed at ending the subjection of women to men'" (Offen, email, 2/5/1997). It was helpful to understand more of the history of feminism in the West by looking at the dictionaries and consulting the experts, but this couldn't sort out the problem of translation. Thus the discussion shifted to the context of China.

In order to show that *nuquan zhuyi* was also a political enterprise, Wang traced the history of feminism in China. She pointed out that feminist thought was being introduced into China at the beginning of the twentieth century. Based on knowledge of the women's suffrage movement in Europe and the United States, *nuquan zhuyi* became the prevailing term when referring to feminism. Men and women who claimed to be progressive and modern were all eager to identify with *nuquan zhuyi*, but why, then, did this term later come to have negative connotations? Wang explained this in the following way:

> The denigration and exclusion of *nuquan zhuyi* was an inseparable part of the CCP's [Chinese Communist Party's] construction of the myth that the CCP was the only saviour of Chinese women. In this very sense, an insistence on the usage of *nuquan zhuyi* would constitute a political gesture that aims at deconstructing the CCP's hegemony of over the discourse of women's liberation.
>
> (Wang, email, 30/4/1997)

But precisely why did *nuxing zhuyi* gain currency in the mid-1980s? Wang proposed the following reason:

> The discourse of femininity emerged in this period with complicated causes. One of them was that women scholars adopted an essentialised notion of women to challenge the dominant category of class. The term *nuxing zhuyi* . . . coming from Taiwan, fitted well with their need at that time to emphasise women's essentialised characteristics and needs.
>
> (Wang, email, 30/4/1997)

Bao, the editor of the 1995 publication, *Collection of Essays on Feminist Scholarship in the West*, disagreed with Wang on several points, asserting that the 'political gesture' of translating the term was actually problematic and would cause problems for women's studies in China:

> I agree that we need to emphasise the political edge of feminism in the contemporary context of China . . . which I believe is extremely important – as we have already stated in our 1995 book. But this is, what is the cause of this loss of women's rights in China? . . . rather than simply focus on the loss of rights, which even in China today, not all women would define in exactly the same way, or agree to the reality that 'women are losing rights in today's China'.
>
> (Bao, email, 30/4/1997)

Another contributor, Xu, argued with Wang about the issue of essentialism in women's studies in China:

> Wang made excellent arguments to link '*nuxing zhuyi*' with the essentialist notion of women. However, I feel your labelling may be only partially correct and may not properly analyse the diverse connotations of '*nuxing zhuyi*' in 1990s China.
>
> (Xu, email, 30/4/1997)

Certainly, the different opinions about *nuxing* between the members of the CSWS had touched upon an important issue, but there were other important questions addressed in this debate, including that of how we should understand the history of Chinese women in the twentieth century. Can we use Western feminist ideas, such as those about essentialism, to label *nuxing zhuyi* in Chinese women's studies? How should we understand the fact that the women's studies scholars and activists prefer this translation?[4] Why had the theoretical debate about *nuxing* arisen in China? Perhaps what is of most consequence here is that the focus and the terms of the debate had shifted from the Western to the Chinese context.

Nuquan zhuyi – in the Western context?
Nuxing zhuyi – in the Chinese context?

This issue was first raised by Su Hongjun in an email in 1997:

> Personally I prefer the latter way, that is to use *nuquan zhuyi* throughout the book because this is what I understand feminism to be in the Western context and how the term is now generally understood in China, from what I know about the Chinese community in women's studies. My impression may be limited, though I have the impression that *nuxing zhuyi* has as an underpinning what some Chinese scholars want to define their 'feminism' as in response to Western 'feminism'.
>
> (Su, email, 28/4/1997)

What draws my attention here is that Su proposes that some Chinese scholars in China were defining feminism as *nuxing zhuyi* in response to Western feminism (*nuquan zhuyi*). That is, for Su, *nuquan zhuyi* and *nuxing zhuyi* were being used as dichotomies. Some contributors were worried that the use of *nuquan zhuyi* to denote Western feminism and *nuxing zhuyi* to denote Chinese feminism would emphasise a division between women and feminists created by the government authorities and some women's studies scholars, and also hinder Chinese women's dialogues with their counterparts in other parts of the world, thereby undermining the growth of feminism in China (Wang, email, 30/4/1997). In response to these points, for instance, Wang suggested that

> valorising *nuquan zhuyi* does not necessarily support the dichotomies between China and West (especially if WE do not use two terms to denote the two phenomena), but could be constructed as a challenge to the dominant discourse as well.
>
> (Wang, email, 30/4/1997)

Indeed, words may be better understood as producers of *effects* than as containers of *meaning* (Rorty, 1989). Wang's statement perhaps implied that the translation used should be directed to producing particular effects in women's studies in China. Moreover, by the use of capitals in 'WE', Wang tried to emphasise that the CSWS occupied a decisive position in such cross-cultural exchanges, while constituting 'WE' as part of an assumed power relationship. I shall also discuss this point later.

Although some contributors to the book were concerned about this issue, they compromised in the end, because they thought it important to see not only the differences, but also the common ground shared with other women throughout the world:

> I would try to put the two together. I have been concerned about these issues for a long time and they are stronger now than they were more than a couple of years ago because it seems this practice has been expanding in China. Although I am concerned about the essentialist connotation within the translation of *nuxing zhuyi*, I do realise the fluidity and complexity of feminism, and plus the fact that Taiwanese scholars and many Chinese scholars are using *nuxing zhuyi* to refer to their ideas. So in my translation, I used *nuquan/nuxing zhuyi*, as a compromise.
>
> (Zhang, N., email, 1/5/1997)

Zhang mentions here that Taiwanese and Chinese scholars were using *nuxing zhuyi* to "refer to their ideas", and not just to 'dichotomise between China and the West'. Could her compromise between *nuquan zhuyi* and *nuxing zhuyi* overcome the problem of dichotomies? Owing to limited time and knowledge, members could not discuss this issue thoroughly by email, but they did agree that "it is extremely important to study the connotations of feminism in the different contexts of China and Taiwan, and also in Hong Kong before and after 1997" (Bao, email, 30/4/1997).

What did the members think about their position in this process of translation? One contributor, Xu, explained her opinion about 'our' (the CSWS) position in this translation event:

> Feminism itself has diverse connotations in the West, historically and contemporarily. Why should we standardise it in Chinese and in this book? If we intend to set up a standard in the theoretical development of feminism in China, I think that we are making a big mistake. Personally, I don't want to be part of it.... Wang mentioned that there have been different translations of the term 'feminism' in China but there is no one book containing different translations. Why cannot our book be the first one?
>
> (Xu, email, 30/4/1997)

Zhang replied with a 'technical' response that, because we are dealing with the same word, contributors should reach agreement to use only one translation for the reader's convenience (Zhang, N., email, 1/5/1997). However, after such a heated debate, most contributors felt that keeping or rejecting the different translations in the book was no longer a technical issue, but a choice which revealed the differences between feminism in the West and in China, and also the different understandings and diverse opinions on feminism in the CSWS. In fact, the members finally reached an agreement, by majority vote, to keep the different translations, and the resultant book was published by the Sanlian Publishing House in 1999.

From this case, we can see that the CSWS was doing translation as an exercise in 'crossing borders'. The discussion concentrated on the definition of the Western context, then moved to the Chinese context, and in addition the differences and diversity of feminism were emphasised. This change, it seems to me, was due to the increasing contact between members of the CSWS and other women in China. Furthermore, this shift in the CSWS's position on translation was no single incident. Throughout the post-colonial era, the focus of translation moved from source language to target language.

My second point, the idea of loss and gain in translation studies, is useful for rethinking the translation of the term feminism: "Once the principle is accepted that sameness cannot exist between two languages, it becomes possible to approach the question of *loss and gain* in the translation process" (Bassnett, 1991: 30). Concerns about 'finding the right word' are perhaps an indication that overseas Chinese scholars have spent so much time discussing what is *lost* in translating the term feminism from English into Chinese that any notion of a potential *gain* has been ignored. It is a puzzle why some members in CSWS worried so much about loss in the translation of the term feminism. Perhaps they thought the Western understanding of the term was the only understanding for the rest of world.

My third point is concerned with 'cultural untranslatability'. After rereading these different opinions about translating the term feminism, the question that I am left with is why some overseas Chinese women's studies scholars thought that the new translation *nuxing zhuyi* presented intellectual problems, including that of essentialism, while women scholars and activists in China welcomed it. An important factor here involves the issue of cultural untranslatability that I noted earlier. When the translation *nuquan zhuyi* was used during the 1980s, it defined the term feminism in the Western context. We, in China, saw it as a Western concept and it was therefore alien to us. When we later found ourselves grappling with the changing political and historical themes of the Western women's movements, while attempting to create a concept to characterise an especially Chinese feminism, the problem of differences between women in China and in the West confronted us. Here, the problem of cultural untranslatability concerns the fundamentally different meanings accorded to the idea of feminism evoked in each cultural context. One interesting example of this concerns the interrogation of the word *zhuyi* (ism) in the CSWS discussions of 1997. Here Chau commented:

> I have the additional problem with the word *zhuyi* as it implies ideological indoctrination, especially after the Chinese people's experience with *makesi zhuyi* (Marxism), *gongchan zhuyi* (communism), etc. . . . therefore, I propose the term *fujie sixiang* (liberate women + thought) for people to consider.
> (Chau, email, 2/5/1997)

No one took up this point, and I think one of the reasons was that after the Cultural Revolution people wanted to keep their distance from the 'old' political term, and they instead preferred a new term that could be accepted as 'depoliticised'. Also, the term 'women's liberation' had been in use in mainland China for years, and translating feminism into this term would only have created more confusion.

Translating 'gender'

In the West, especially in North America, the term 'gender' has played a key role in feminist theory and politics since the late 1960s. The term gender is usually taken to have an Anglo-American origin, and it has sometimes been reviled as one of those expressions 'made in the USA'. Debates over its meaning reflect major turning points in feminist thinking over the past 30 years. "Even here, though, there was no fixed meaning beyond the idea of 'social sex'", wrote Joan Scott. "There were feminists who took sexual difference as given, the ground on which gender systems were then built; there were others who took sexual difference to be the effect of historically variable discursive practices of 'gender'" (Scott, 2003: 13).

Compared with the term feminism, the term gender has even more linguistic troubles attached to it. Historically, gender has been in use in the English language from the late thirteenth century. It denoted the grammatical classification of various types of substantives of the feminine or masculine sex. "The capacity for gender to mean both classificatory difference, as in its grammatical sense, learned masculine and feminine behaviours, copulation, and non-heteronormative sexual acts is retained in the conflicting and overlapping uses of gender today" (Olson, 2012). It is one important reason for offering an easy definition of gender. Along the same lines, in defining gender as a keyword in a German Marxist dictionary, Donna Haraway started her entry as follows:

> The root of the English, French, and Spanish words is the Latin verb, *generare*, to beget, and the Latin stem *gener-*, race or kind. An obsolete English meaning of 'to gender' is 'to copulate' (Oxford English Dictionary). The substantives 'Geschlecht', 'gender', 'genre', and 'genero' refer to the notion of sort, kind and class. . . . The modern English and German words, 'gender' and 'Geschlecht', adhere closely to concepts of sex, sexuality, sexual difference, generation, engendering, and so on, while the French and Spanish seem not to carry those meanings as readily. Words close to 'gender' are implicated in concepts of kinship, race, biological taxonomy, language, and nationality.
>
> (Haraway, 1991: 130)

This complex linguistic history of the term gender in European languages indicates that the translation of this term from English into other languages will invariably be difficult.

Returning to the political side of the discussion, the debate over gender that preceded the 1995 FWCW revealed certain issues concerning power that can influence translation matters. During the preparations for the Beijing conference, the Vatican and other conservative forces made a serious attempt to undermine feminism by staging an apparently trivial attack on the use of the word gender. The Vatican attacked what it believed to be the very foundation of feminist theory: gender, interpreted as a socially constructed difference between feminine and masculine. The preparatory document for the Beijing conference used the term gender to refer to the difference between masculine and feminine as distinct from anatomical sex, but not as a euphemism for sexual orientation as the critics suggested. Jean Franco (1998) has argued that the Vatican's attack was not only 'against' feminism, but also 'for' presenting the Church as a bulwark against the 'savage capitalist'. This was aided by the fact that the Spanish and Portuguese word for gender, *genero*, did not have the same range of meanings as in English.

From this point of departure, I now want to reconsider these issues in the light of my detailed examination of the process by which the term gender travelled to China, where the term departed from, how it travelled, how it was received and by whom, which translations of it were produced, and how these were received in different cultural and political contexts in China.

To start with we must understand that the story of the term gender travelling to China is quite different, and in a political sense it has had a much easier journey than the term feminism. Although the word gender had been translated into Chinese, and a gender perspective had been mentioned in some articles in China during the 1980s, not many people had noticed that a new concept was involved until the 1993 workshop on "Chinese Women and Development" at Tianjin Normal University in China. At this workshop, the idea of a gender perspective was introduced by a group of Chinese scholars from the CSWS where it became the focus of discussion. Since then, gender as a social category and a concept has been central to women's studies in China (Zhang with Xu, 1995). In consequence, gender theory has been widely accepted among members of the ACWF, Chinese women's studies scholars, and activists since the FWCW in 1995.

Translating 'gender': **xingbie** *or* **shehui xingbie**

In the years after the word gender had gained acceptance, divergent views emerged on its proper translation, and thus the word's actual meaning. Having no equivalent in the Chinese language, the term gender had been translated into *xingbie* (literally, 'sexual difference') since the 1980s. *Xingbie* is already a part of the Chinese vocabulary and using it to translate the term gender was an easy way to help people understand this imported word. A new translation, *shehui xingbie* (social + sexual difference), came into existence and found widespread acceptance in the middle of the 1990s. *Shehui xingbie* is a created word in which translators try to add new meaning. Compared with the debates concerning the translation of the term feminism, discussion about translating the term gender into Chinese has been much less heated (Wang, Z., 1997b; Li, X., 1999b; 2002).

Gender: translation as **xingbie**

Women's studies scholar Li Xiaojiang is among those who have argued most cogently for translating gender as *xingbie* rather than *shehui xingbie*. According to Li, it is not difficult to define the concepts sex and gender in the Chinese language because the term 'sex' (*xing*) refers to the natural element, while the term 'gender' (*xingbie*) refers to social identity. Until now, whether or not we like to face up to it, the natural and the social aspects of gender have been coexistent (2002). In order to prove her point, she draws on features of the Chinese language:

> The terms *woman* (*nuren*) and *man* (*nanren*) already reveal their social character, since they refer to 'human beings who have a socialised sexual character'. At the same time, both the terms *nu* (female) and *nan* (male) are attached to the term *human being* (*ren*), whereas the English word *woman* is attached to the word *man*. Therefore, in China, no matter how far women's liberation is carried out, there is no need to launch another revolution in our conceptual scheme, because in our language the term *woman* (*nuren*) is not predicated on *man*. Furthermore, if it were not for the sake of facilitating communication between China and the West, it would be redundant to introduce the notion of gender (*shehui xingbie*) to the Chinese language, since *nu* and *nan* are already understood as social, and not natural, beings.
>
> (Li, X., 1999b: 262)

As a pioneer of women's studies in China, Li has always been concerned to maintain the difference existing between Chinese women and women in the West, and anxious that Chinese women's studies does not lose itself in the lure of 'connecting with the international track'. In trying to stick to using an already existing Chinese term to translate gender, Li has, in effect, given up the chance of reinterpreting the old word *xingbie*. Perhaps Li's attitude towards Western feminism can be defined as a defensive position, in which a language practice acknowledges the otherness and opposes the other (Robyns, 1994). This defensive posture "enhances its specificity by heavily emphasizing the otherness of the 'alien' discourse" (1994: 67). Consequently, "translation is generally viewed in a negative light" (1994: 68), or in other words, Li's defensive position was a position from which to refuse to translate the dominant concept from the West.

In terms of language, Li overlooks the fact that the Chinese language has changed a great deal since the turn of the twentieth century, due to translations and the unavoidable adoption of Western terms and ideas. An interesting example of this is the adoption of gender markers in written Chinese. As Lydia H. Liu's research has revealed, one of the most fascinating neologisms invented in this period was the gendering of the third-person pronoun in written Chinese. The original form of the Chinese character for the pronoun *ta* contains an engendered *ren* (denoting the human species), and the gendering of this pronoun arose from circumstances of translation of English, French, and other European languages. "Such a split at the symbolic level of the pronoun allows gender to shape social relations of power in a new language" (Liu, L., 1995).

Moreover, Liu's research enables a methodological rethinking of translingual representation of gender in modern China. Rather than refusing to adopt the new concepts, Liu links them to broader ideas about change:

> In a broader sense, deictic constructions of gender reflect and participate in a larger gendering process under way since the turn of the twentieth century, as Chinese men, women, and the state discover separately for themselves and in terms of one another that they all have a stake in deciding how gender difference should be constructed and what kind of political investment that difference should or could represent in China's pursuit of modernity.
>
> (Liu, L., 1995: 38–39)

Perhaps the important point here is that instead of refusing translation, we have to understand first what the translation is. Indeed, through translation, one can broaden knowledge and experience of the world, "in such a way as to 'better evaluate which alternatives are possible and are available today'" (Ribeiro, 2004: 194). This thinking has to be based on a sense of post-colonial translation.

Gender: translation as shehui xingbie

Another important argument on the translation of the term gender came from the overseas Chinese scholar Wang Zheng. As a key figure in the promotion of gender theory in China, Wang strongly recommended that the translation should be *shehui xingbie* (social + sexual difference). In her article "An Analysis of 'Female Consciousness' and 'Gender Consciousness'", Wang briefly introduces the history of gender theory in the West, mainly in the United States. Her view is that, compared with the theory of gender and in particular the ideas of Gayle Rubin (1975) and Joan Scott (1988), the translation *xingbie* does not satisfactorily render the meaning that gender has in Western feminism. *Xingbie* derives from and 'fits' Chinese culture, and confining gender to *xingbie* not only limits our understanding but also makes the concept confusing. For Wang, translations should avoid using terms which are full of existing ideas because this packs too much into the new concept, and she therefore argues that gender should be translated as *shehui xingbie* (Wang, Z., 1997b). For Wang, this is sound translation strategy: because the new term is made up of two words (social and sexual difference), it will make people ask "what is *shehui xingbie*?" This question is a good starting point for understanding the new term (Wang, Z., 1997b).

Perhaps Wang Zheng was right, and *xingbie* constitutes a good example of helpful 'unfaithful translation'. Indeed, it is hard to read it as incorporating the meanings commented on by Gayle Rubin (1975) or Joan Scott (1988). As a major translator of gender theories into Chinese, Wang Zheng closely followed the debate over how to convey the sense of Western feminist ideas and concepts to Chinese readers in an accurate fashion. Wang wished to use gender theory as a heuristic device for producing better knowledge for women's and gender studies in China. However, anyone engaged in this quest would inevitably come face-to-face with the hegemony of the source system.

If we accept that a major concept can never be precisely and entirely translated from one language into another, then it is clear that "to seek for 'exact' translation and 'exact' definition is not only wrongheadedness, but also leads to muddled analyses and muddled arguments" (Overing, 1987: 76). The question is, instead, how to better understand translation itself. Perhaps the important thing to hang on to is that "it is not the 'word' that we must translate, but another way of understanding things about the world that we must comprehend and *learn*" (Overing, 1987: 76).

I agree with Liu that rather than arguing about how to properly translate the term gender into Chinese,

> one might do well to focus on the ways in which intellectual resources from the West and from China's past are cited, translated, appropriated, or claimed in moments of perceived historical contingency so that something called *change* may be produced. In my view, this change is always different from China's own past and from the West, but have profound linkages with both.
>
> (Liu, L., 1995: 39)

What needs to be grasped is the 'what' and 'why' of the translation *xingbie* or *shehui xingbie* in the particular framework in which it is used, and how this relates to the political and cultural situation of China.

Interpreting 'gender'

In 1998, when I was writing my master's thesis on translation, it had been five years since the term gender was introduced into China at the Tianjin workshop in 1993, and since then both *xingbie* and *shehui xingbie* had been used for the term gender in the Chinese language. In my thesis, I pointed out that although Gayle Rubin's and Joan Scott's works on gender had been translated into Chinese, and a large number of books and articles on the theory of gender had also been published in China, using gender as a category to analyse society, history, and culture was still rare (Lin, C., 1997; Min, 1998). As Lin Chun commented, "To what extent the new word can be articulated in the Chinese language and context as a useful category remains to be seen" (Lin, C., 1997: 18). Indeed, how to interpret the concept of gender and use gender as a category of analysis in the Chinese context remained an open question. With this puzzle in my mind, I started my fieldwork in China in 1999.

In Beijing, I was given articles on women's studies and gender in China by Liu Bohong and Li Huiying, two of the most prominent advocates of 'channelling *xingbie* (gender) consciousness into the mainstream of policy-making'. These two articles provide some important clues about the interpretation of gender.

In Liu Bohong's (1999) article, she claims that the introduction of gender theory into China implies a 'revolutionary meaning'. Liu describes three different aspects of the *xingbie* (gender) perspective in China:

- The *xingbie* perspective as standing for equality between women and men;
- Channelling the *xingbie* perspective into the mainstream of policy-making;
- *Xingbie* as an analytic category.

Perhaps due to her position in the ACWF, Liu had been one of the key persons responsible for translating the documents passed from the UN and other international organisations to the ACWF and other women's and gender studies groups. Liu tried to mix the gender perspective and Marxist theory of women, promoting in particular the development of gender theory in China. However, this is a rather neutral approach to the interpretation of gender.

Interestingly, in her article Li Huiying (1999) strongly criticised the 'misinterpretation' of the term gender by the ACWF, associating this with two points: the ACWF's taking the individual subjective consciousness out of the *xingbie* consciousness and the ACWF's blurring the distinction between the *xingbie* consciousness and Marxist theory of women (Li, H., 1999). Li Huiying explained these points in my interview with her:

> The *xingbie* consciousness includes a gender perspective. When it came from the West, it embodied the meaning that everybody has their own rights and dignity, and it also emphasised that people are independent and have initiative. But *xingbie* as the ACWF interpreted it is just the difference between men and women, but didn't consider the rights which men and women should both have, but presently do not, to be an independent person. They dismissed this aspect of gender. Women and men, rather than being treated as individual persons, have been equally treated as a kind of 'tool' by the government. For example, population policy takes women as a 'tool' of reproduction. It is impossible to let the ACWF question this for it will affect the policy of the state. The ACWF had to find a meeting point with the government. Gender was misinterpreted by the ACWF, but this is an unavoidable thing in China.
>
> (interview, Min/Li, 3/3/1999)

Li Huiying's comments here show how the relationship between Chinese women, the ACWF, and the government could be affected by the translation of the term gender in China. This particular interpretation of gender is based on the view that in the West, gender theory equates with individual rights. Although one could argue that gender theory means something else in the West, the point I am making is that its travelling in China changes its meanings. Sometimes, the term gender has been used as a synonym for feminism.

While Li Huiying was criticising the ACWF's misunderstanding of the meaning of gender, ironically she did not see that something similar could be said about the approach of women's studies scholars in general. The ACWF also needed a new interpretation and new language in these times of change, and gender theory offered them the possibility of dialogue both outside and inside China, in a way which included both Marxist theory of women (past) and *xingbie* (present). Although Li disagreed with the interpretation of gender by the ACWF, she still recognised that "the ACWF, mixing up *xingbie* consciousness and Marxism, turned on a green light for channelling gender perspectives into the mainstream of policy-making and to spread the term throughout mainland China" (Li, H., 1999: 2). In this situation, Li proposed:

> Rather than clarify the concept of gender interpreted by the ACWF, we could borrow the power from them to promote channelling *shehui xingbie* consciousness into the mainstream of policy-making . . . Alternatively, we could develop research on gender; write and edit training books on gender . . . Through the spreading of the *shehui xingbie* perspective we can influence policy making and the social development model in government.
>
> (Li, H., 1999: 4)

The third opinion on the interpretation of gender is that gender is a form of power. One of my interviewees told me:

> My understanding of gender is quite brave. Gender is a structure of power. The issue of politics and law includes power and right. Gender is power. Only with power can you have rights. If you want a right, you must strive for power. You can use gender either academically or politically. It is a vital power.
>
> (interview, Min/Du, 7/4/1999)

The word 'power' was repeated over and over in Du's remarks. Even though she is not an English speaker, she used English terms when she mentioned the words gender, power and rights in order to emphasise their 'original' meaning. For her and other Chinese women's studies scholars, gender theory does indeed afford power, for by promoting gender theory these scholars receive political, academic, and financial resources previously beyond their reach. Consequently,

I was curious that the term gender seemed to be a substitute for the term feminism. Gao Xiaoxian's explanation bore this out:

> I take gender as a part of feminism and don't divide them into two parts. Gender theory offers me a very useful viewpoint to deconstruct the old theory and phenomena in traditional culture.
>
> (interview, Min/Gao, 14/7/1999)

In Kunming, Zhao Jie, a feminist researcher who works on the issues of gender and development, made a similar point in more forceful terms:

> In our gender studies group, most members would like to accept gender, but not feminism. I have argued with them on this issue. I think feminism concerns the social relationship behind the gender relationship, and involves questioning why women and men are different. That is why I think feminism and gender should be joined together. One of the members of our group asked, 'Is it because feminism has become a dead end that they talk about gender?' I don't think so.
>
> (interview, Min/Zhao, 30/3/1999)

I see gender as an analytic category that has an incongruous history in China. On the one hand, it was a useful concept for the ACWF and in women's studies academic circles as a means of deconstructing the old discourse of Marxist theory of women and opening up new ways to tackle issues of discrimination. On the other hand, in many places the use of the category of gender meant only a change of label, not of content. For some academics, gender studies was more appealing in the sense that they could continue to do women's studies without running the risk of it being called feminism. Perhaps the trend of the depoliticisation of academic feminism should be noted as a very marked feature of the broad changes occurring within women's studies.

In order to get rid of sexual essentialism in Chinese women's studies, the distinction between sex and gender was emphasised by these translations. In the end, gender became a dominant word in women's studies circles. For example, at the end of 2001, I received an academic exchange proposal in both English and Chinese from the women's studies centre at a university in China. In this, the term gender was translated as 'social gender'. I would guess that this translation came from the Chinese *shehui xingbie* (social + sexual difference). It could be argued that this Chinese translator was unfamiliar with Western feminism, and that she (or he) was unaware of the debates occurring on the distinction between sex and gender in the West. But the point I wish draw from this example is very different: because of the lack of feminist discussions and debates on the relationship between sex and gender when gender theory travelled to

China and was translated into Chinese, it lost its original meanings. The term gender became simply another word for sex, and thus the need for my feminist correspondent to qualify it as *social* gender in the exchange proposal. Another interesting aspect is that an earlier body of literature on this issue was completely ignored. Since the 1980s, a number of feminist social scientists have challenged the distinction between sex and gender by asserting that sex itself is a social construction (Jackson, 1999). It may be that this other work primarily grew out of European social science and was not known to scholars of the CSWS in the United States. Still, the puzzle remains: what political and economic machine legitimated particular uses of language in the Chinese women's movement while delegitimising other uses?

What we have to learn, I think, from these various interpretations of gender, is that

> ideas and concepts – which are never totally 'pure' or 'native' – flow out from locations that are already imbricated with other places and saturated by other ideas and concepts and subjects of enunciation, therefore opening up routes that attend closely to a rhizomatic logic: there is no clear point of origin nor an unequivocal end point.
>
> (Costa, 2001: 2)

So why is it that gender was so extremely influential in the 1990s in women's studies and in the women's movement in China (sometimes even superseding the term feminism)? In addition to the political needs of the ACWF, I think there are two primary reasons. The first is that *xingbie* is an old word which means 'sexual difference' in Chinese, and this fitted well with the emerging understanding of the differences between the two sexes in China. However, employing the concept of difference in the absence of critics would not only lead to the essentialisation of 'natural difference', but would also help us move away from the aim of fighting for a feminist perspective on equality and justice. The second reason is that it was linked with the revival of traditional Chinese culture, which has always emphasised *harmony* between the two sexes, and here some women's studies scholars argued that the idea of *xingbie* consciousness could be used to promote the coordinated development of the sexes, thus making conflict between them unnecessary. In short, by not directly questioning capitalism and men's oppression of women, the gender discourse may have helped render invisible the question of power in the massive economic and social transition in China.

Are there problems and limits in terms of transnational feminism? The questions relating to the translation of gender across borders have been addressed by many writers. As Greta Olson has pointed out, "Gender's post-1990s travels have in fact created points of dissonance and dissatisfaction in terms of the politics, the path of intellectual inquiry, and the institutional acceptance of feminism" (Olson, 2012: 10). We have heard that gender replaced feminism in the Brazilian academic context (Costa, 2000); gender replaced women in the Swedish context (Liinason, 2011); and something similar happened in China. "Such a shift, one can assume, explains why in many universities theoretical feminism is reduced to an intellectual project of understanding women in their individuality or specificity, rather than as a group or as a socio-political class" (Descarries, 2003: 629). With the term gender in hand, it seemed that issues of gender and women could be studied without engaging in a feminist political project. The term gender appeared – to some – to be a neutral concept with no need of political theorising. Such views were among the seeds which would depoliticise women's and gender studies in the 1990s.[5]

Ruminations: questions and challenges

In my investigation of how the two terms feminism and gender were translated into Chinese during the 1980s to 1990s, I came to the conclusion that translation in the broad sense is a process of negotiating meaning, for

> meaning is not located within the culture itself but in the process of negotiation which is part of its continual reactivation. The solutions to many of the translator's dilemmas are not to be found in Dictionaries, but rather in an understanding of the way language is tied to local realities, to literary forms and to changing identities. . . . In fact the process of meaning transfer often has less to do with *finding* the culture inscription of a term than in *reconstructing* its value.
> (Simon, 1996: 138)

As I did this research, I noticed that one of the problems involved in writing the history of such translations is the common misreading of feminism as unitary and intrinsically Western. The standard narrative is that feminism developed out of Western thought, and now 'it' is spreading to other countries and cultures. This dominant narrative conceives of the power of the flow of ideas as unidirectional, but it omits power relationships from its account of travelling.

My second point relates to the issue of the translator. Once translation is no longer treated as an invisible practice, the figure of the translator emerges from the shadows, and can be seen as an active agent within the translation processes. As Bassnett has noted,

> By studying translator's prefaces we can learn a great deal not only about the criteria selected by an individual translator, but about the ways in which those criteria reflect views on the task of translation held within the community at large.
> (Bassnett, 1991: xiii)

The translators who were involved in the process of dialogue and negotiation in the translation of feminism and gender came from three different sets of interests.

First is the ACWF. The ACWF is involved in making official discourse, and it is moreover a nationwide organisation, and so it still occupies a decisive position in the negotiation of such translations (although this has been increasingly questioned). In the 1980s, the dilemma that the ACWF faced was whether to give priority to the interests of women or to the interests of the Communist Party and government. The ACWF needed to find a new theory and a new language to deal with conflicts between traditional Marxist theory of women and a recognition of current discriminatory practices. Although the ACWF adopted some liberal feminist ideas from abroad, it still avoided the term feminism. In the 1990s, when the idea of a gender perspective was channelled into China through UN official documents from the FWCW, the ACWF quickly changed its position and accepted the notion of a gender perspective. The term gender (*xingbie*) has since underpinned a new language which fits with Marxist theory of women. However, limited by the current political structure, which dims the prospects for dialogue, the ACWF has had to slow down its translation efforts.

The other translator involved in the process of dialogue and negotiation was the scholars and activists of women's and gender studies, who were the key presence in the process of translating the terms feminism and gender. With the increasingly frequent dialogues between feminists abroad and feminists in China, the interpretation and understanding of these terms has greatly influenced the direction and nature of the women's movement in China. The translation of the term feminism and debates revolving around this have shown how Chinese feminism has evolved by engaging with both its similarities to and differences from Western feminism. Because most Chinese women's studies scholars and activists do not use English and have no access to English academic resources, they have to rely on translated information (second-hand translation) to enter into dialogue with their foreign colleagues. This imbues the choice of 'who' and 'what' is translated – and is thus able to travel – with even greater significance.

The third translator involved was the CSWS. Most members of the CSWS are Chinese scholars or students living in the United States, in addition to a small contingent living in other Western countries. When women's studies was establishing itself in China in the middle of the 1980s, many members of the CSWS went to the United States, and much of their knowledge of feminism and women's studies was gained there. In this sense, CSWS members are located at the borders between cultures, and their acts of translation aim at crossing these borders. This involves a new speaking position for the CSWS, which the organisation has attempted to fulfil through projects such as publishing translated feminist books and organising workshops and conferences on women's studies and women and development. However, and returning to my earlier point about the power relations which inform contemporary cultural exchanges, a different interpretation of this is that members of the CSWS are living in the First World (United States) and not in Third World countries; therefore, their location is one of privilege. For instance, the CSWS was a very important element in the process of translating key works of gender theory into Chinese. Most of the literature they have translated comes from the United States, with very little from elsewhere. However, with the growth of women's and gender studies in China, the CSWS gradually lost its privileged position.

This brings me to my third point, which is concerned with the power relationship between travelling theory and cultural translation. Indeed, Chinese women's studies scholars and activists are always eager to learn about Western feminism, but they rarely question or challenge the dominance of Western knowledge.

The ACWF and scholars and activists of women studies employed the idea of *jiegui* to challenge existing internal hegemonies, and to assert that global and Western feminist ideas represented advanced, progressive thought. In the meantime, this blocked any questioning of who and what represented the global and the international community, hindered exploration of the limits of global feminism, and prevented thinking more critically about just which Western feminisms travelled and why. We have to remember, however, that "contemporary transnational feminist flows of ideas and interactions, however, are not always analytically sophisticated in helping us chart this world of overlapping identities and scattered hegemonies" (True, 1999: 285).

What became lost in the process of translation were not just thoughts and experiences from outside the United States, but also the insights of critics for those translations. As pointed out by several feminist scholars, this led to a problematic situation, in which the concept of gender became omnipresent in women's studies, while too few questions were raised about the theoretical justification for using the term across dissimilar linguistic environments. The president of the Free University of Women in Milan asserted in 2000: "Now that the concept of gender has succeeded in imposing itself everywhere in the American academy and in developing agencies of the Third World, we can start measuring the extent of the high cost of analytical richness lost" (Paola Melchiori, 2000, quoted from Descarries, 2003: 629).

The dialogue involved in translating the terms feminism and gender into Chinese is not only related to a dialogue with transnational feminism – which is in turn related to the agendas of both international agencies and funding facilities – it is also related to a dialogue with Marxist theory of women in China. Considering that Marxist theory of women was upheld as the guiding principle of the Women's Federation in the 1990s, the other challenge was that of constructing an updated version of socialist feminist thought and action, which could be founded on debates about the intertwining of discrimination and inequality. Although from the 1990s, Marxist theory of women was re-evaluated with reference to socialist feminism and liberal feminism by the Women's Federation, the dialogue between Marxist theory of women and the theory of gender and other feminisms did not occur in Chinese women's studies circles in the 1990s. This dialogue did, however, begin to take place after 2010.

Notes

1 However, the introduction most Chinese intellectuals had to Western thought was mediated through Japan. See the research by Sudo (2007).
2 For instance, I interviewed 18 scholars and activists in my fieldwork in 1999; 17 of them had experiences gained from their time as participants at conferences and visiting women's studies organisations abroad during the 1990s. Of course, no country had received as many of them as visitors as had the United States.
3 Because I was not able to access the Internet at that time, I was unable to become involved in this debate, although I did receive copies of the email discussions by post.
4 I do think that some members of the CSWS did not fully understand the history of women's studies in China during the 1980s. Instead of learning from women's studies scholars and activists in China, they generalised that Chinese women's studies had adopted essentialism since the 1980s and did not ask why. See my discussion of this issue in Chapter 2.
5 I will come back to this issue in Chapter 6.

4 *Jiegui* (connecting with the international track)
The 1990s

> The railway tracks in Russia and Inner Mongolia are different gauges from each other. Consequently, at the border, passengers, goods or whatever have to change trains to enable further travel. What is it that we call jiegui? The train, wherever it travels, needs a constant track gauge that is the same axle width as its wheels. Therefore, if the 'tracks', for instance in the East and the West are different gauges the train then cannot travel further.
>
> (interview, Min/Gao, 14/7/1999)

After 1989, China experienced several years of political upheaval and economic depression. In 1992 China's paramount leader at the time, Deng Xiaoping, toured southern China to instil new momentum into his reform programme. In order to get past the shadow of the events of Tiananmen Square in 1989, Deng Xiaoping made a series of political pronouncements designed to reinvigorate the process of economic reform. The 14th Party Congress later in that year backed Deng's renewed push for market reforms, stating that the development plan for the 1990s would stress continuity in the political system amid bolder reforms in the economic realm.

However, the shift from the state socialist system to a market economy caused a series of political and social problems. Furthermore, in terms of gender, a new class inequality combined with gender stratification had intensified throughout the country since the 1990s. Major gaps developed among women from different classes with respect to education, wages, social status, social security, and so forth, although gender differences continued to exist at various social levels. A highly gendered society had emerged. As Lin Chun noted,

> Reforms are failing women (along with workers and farmers), as evidenced by high unemployment, poor labour conditions, lack of protection for rural migrants, the commercialisation (and traditionalisation according to artificial 'Oriental taste') of femininity, and ultimately the erasure of the problem of gender inequality.
>
> (Lin, C., 2001: 1284)

As China's modernisation programme increasingly converged with global capitalism, its problems became much more complex. The reforms referred to earlier led to the complete incorporation of China's economic and cultural life into a global market, but after some time the state was less and less able to adapt and reform itself, especially with regard to political and social reforms. However, as other changes proceeded apace, a good many far-reaching changes occurred which had consequences for political power and the structures through which it operated. It was against this background that the new term *jiegui* (connecting with the international track) emerged as a metaphor reflecting an enthusiastic attitude towards globalisation. *Jiegui* was based on the view that China had been an outsider to the international community (the international track) for a long time – and when China returned to the international community, it had to change its gauge to fit the international track. The women's movement and women's studies was one of the fields which experienced significant transformation as a consequence of *jiegui*.

New concepts and ideas from UN-based transnational feminisms first trickled into China with the Fourth World Conference on Women (FWCW) and the NGO Forum of 1995. According to the (incomplete) statistics, over 100 women's studies conferences were held; more than 30 new women's studies centres were set up in academic circles; and over 150 books and 2,000 articles on women's issues were published in China between 1993 and 1998 (Liu, B., 1999). The new flow of transnational feminist and women's and gender studies[1] ideas had become a major source of analytical tools which could be used by Chinese women's studies researchers and activists. This movement constituted a second major wave of translations of Western feminism.

The new metaphor, *jiegui*, found wide usage among Chinese women, reflecting their enthusiasm for the transnational feminisms. However, what did *jiegui* mean in Chinese political discourse in the 1990s? What attitude was there to *jiegui* in the All China Women's Federation (ACWF) and academic women's studies groups? Precisely who were we going to connect with? How would this connecting actually take place? What particular ideas were being received through *jiegui*? These questions puzzled me and other researchers from the middle of the 1990s (see Wang, Z., 1997a; Hsiung and Wong, 1998; Li, X., 2000b; Spakowski, 2001; Xu, 2009). These are also the questions that this chapter intends to open up. Treating *jiegui* as a metaphor, I hope to convey some of the concerns of this exciting time in Chinese feminism by tracing the emergence of different attitudes and approaches towards transnational feminisms in the Women's Federation and in academic circles. First, I will focus on attitudes towards *jiegui* among different groups of Chinese women by discussing the narratives of women's studies scholars and activists and of the ACWF. Then I will examine why and how particular ideas, such as the non-governmental organisation (NGO) and 'doing a project' travelled through externally funded projects into Chinese women's and gender studies and reshaped the field significantly.

The attitudes toward *jiegui* (connecting with the international track)

One of the major events in this process of *jiegui* was China's hosting of the 1995 Fourth World Conference on Women (FWCW). It was the first time since 1949 that a massive women's group from around the world had a chance to meet Chinese women.

According to the official narrative of the ACWF, the organisation had engaged with the outside world ever since the first UN World Conference on Women in 1975. However, the ACWF's outside contact was mediated by the state, shaped by the official ideology of the Chinese Communist Party (CCP) on women's issues, and subject to the political and diplomatic needs of the country (Zhang and Hsiung, 2010). It might be said that the UN World Conference on Women had little relevance for the lives of Chinese women, except for a few officials in the ACWF and in the Chinese government.

It was in 1991 that the Chinese government made the decision to host the FWCW. Although this decision quite possibly rested mainly on political expediency following Tiananmen Square in 1989, it nevertheless had some immediate positive effects on the lives of women and also brought with it some unexpected results.

Most of the Chinese women's studies scholars and activists that I interviewed very much welcomed the idea of *jiegui*. One of the leading scholars of women's studies, Li Huiying, said that "for China, the most important thing is to 'open the door', and continue the communication with the world. It doesn't matter even if we are not similar at all" (interview, Min/Li, 3/3/1999). Dai Jinhua, one of the leading Chinese feminist scholars, also spoke favourably about the FWCW: "As a turning point, suddenly the FWCW opened a window for us, we saw a new world. In fact, the process of preparation for the FWCW was a process of dissemination of feminism in China" (Dai, 1999: 153). It is noteworthy that Li and Dai use 'door' and 'window' as metaphors to emphasise their desire to escape the confinement of political control and officialdom after the events of Tiananmen Square and breathe fresh air from the outside world.

These positive attitudes towards *jiegui* represented an important political trend in China in the 1990s. Many things changed at the official level as well. After government officials from all over the world signed the *Platform for Action* at the FWCW, the ACWF was quick to use the pledge made by the Chinese government. The ACWF launched a nationwide campaign to implement the *Platform for Action* and the *Beijing Declaration*, the two documents that 'voice the aspiration of women all over the world'. This campaign, though mainly picked up by the Women's Federation, helped create legitimacy for the Chinese women's movement. However, in terms of 'connecting with the international track', the ACWF had to work out how to combine the term 'gender' with traditional Marxist theory of women and how to adapt to the concept of the NGO in place of their old organisational structure.

In November 1996, the president of the ACWF, Chen Muhua, produced a new exposition of Marxist theory of women. She emphasised that "Marxist women's theory is concerned to analyse women's issues from a gender (*xingbie*) perspective, and its core is the equality between men and women" (see Yiying and Yihong, 1998). The intent on the part of the ACWF was to incorporate these new ideas into the old theories so as to keep abreast of political and economic changes and to connect with the international community. The new exposition was an official encouragement to import new ideas, as well as an indication that gender was becoming a popular concept in official discourse. Gradually, the concept of 'equality between men and women' became 'gender equality' in the discourse of the Women's Federation and women's studies in academic circles.

But if there was no difference between the old theory of equality between men and women and the new term gender (*xingbie*), as the leaders of the ACWF indicated, then why should the ACWF need the term gender in their discourse? Was gender, as a new term, really useful, or was it included just for propaganda purposes? To address this confusion and satisfy my own mind, I reread the report of the special symposium that discussed the issue of gender (*xingbie*) consciousness which had been held by the Women's Studies Centre of the Central Party's Cadres School in 1996. Scholars of women's studies, activists, and women officers from the ACWF and from the central government all participated in this meeting.

The first point addressed at the meeting was to ask whether *xingbie* consciousness was needed in China. The answer, it was agreed, was 'yes', and two reasons were emphasised by various participants. One reason was that there was a lack of *xingbie* consciousness in China; the other reason was the inequality that existed between men and women in China. Taken together, these two reasons meant that *xingbie* consciousness had to be introduced in our society (Li, H., 1996). But how did the participants account for this, considering that the official discourse still focused on equality between men and women? Kang Ling, the secretary of the ACWF secretariat, argued that even though the laws and policies in China reflected equality between the two sexes generally, this was no guarantee that discrimination against women could not occur in practice. For instance, the ACWF had raised the issue of women's education with the Department of Education in the central government. The Department of Education asserted that it was not necessary to address this issue because women and men had equal rights to education. For Kang Ling, the argument was that, although there was no discriminative clause in the law, this did not ensure that women and men received equal treatment in practice. As a consequence, the idea took root that *xingbie* consciousness could help to eliminate forms of discrimination against women (Li, H., 1996). In this way, Kang Ling's statement also helped to explain why the word *xingbie* consciousness was useful to the ACWF at that time.

In the larger context, the socio-economic transformation was proceeding rapidly, and the ACWF had to deal with the conflict between traditional Marxist theory of women and the widespread recognition that women were being discriminated against in practice. The ACWF leadership consequently needed a new language with which to address women's and gender issues within the framework of Marxist theory of women. It seemed that the concept of gender (*xingbie*) provided a new term that helped the ACWF to solve its problem. Although officially the ACWF emphasised that *xingbie* consciousness and equality between the two sexes amounted to exactly the same thing, the difference was that *xingbie* consciousness takes as a starting point the *a priori* recognition of inequality between women and men, while traditional Marxist theory of women has a blind spot regarding *xingbie*.

This still leaves the question of why the ACWF had changed its attitude towards transnational feminism so much and so quickly, particularly with regard to the concept of gender. A leading women's studies scholar in the ACWF suggested the following explanation:

> The ACWF always follows the government. If the Chinese government has an agreement about the *Platform for Action*, that means they should also recognise the gender perspective. Therefore the ACWF grasped the opportunity to introduce the gender perspective. In the meantime, the ACWF wanted to raise the status of the organization. If gender consciousness is being channelled into mainstream policy-making, then the ACWF as an organization will be joining the political mainstream.
> (interview, Min/Liu, 5/3/1999)

As noted, the power relationship between ACWF and the state had changed since the FWCW was held in Beijing. The Chinese government treated the FWCW as not just an event for women, but also as an opportunity to reap nationalist publicity. The ACWF wanted to use this opportunity to promote the women's movement, and the accommodating attitude of the government made it much easier for the concept of gender to travel to China.

If the ACWF continued to keep the term gender as a *useful* term, then they might also use it to 'translate' Marxist theory of women into a new approach. However, the incorporation of feminist claims at the level of official UN and government policy do not necessarily translate into effective implementation. As the development of a market economy became a more dominant issue, the issue of women was demoted and few resources were allocated to promoting gender equality. In fact, the head of the ACWF would not agree to insert the term 'gender' into the documents of the 8th National Congress in 1998 (interview, Min/Liu, 5/3/1999). Thus, the chasm between these ideas, domestic politics and actual practice in China remained.

Nevertheless, in a specifically political sense, *xingbie* consciousness was still widely used in official ACWF discourse and by many women's studies scholars and activists (Liu, B., 1999; Gao, Jiang, and Wang, 2002). Gender-oriented projects are continued by the ACWF and local women's federations. For example, the women's federation in Yunnan Province has conducted three large gender-training workshops for their cadres since the year 2000. Since then, gender mainstreaming has become a common discourse among the cadres of the Women's Federation of Yunnan, as I found out when I interviewed several of them in Kunming in 2003.

Two factors were crucial in the process of importing transnational feminism into China, the first being the projects of gender and development. It is no surprise that transnational links around 'development' funding played a fundamental role in pushing Chinese women's studies into particular ways of connecting with the international track in the 1990s (Du, 1996, 2001; Wang, Z., 1997a; Hsiung and Wong, 1998; Li, X., 2000b; Spakowski, 2001; Milwertz, 2002; Xu, 2009). An important part was played by international organisations and Western foundations, such as the Ford Foundation, UNIFEM (United Nations Development Fund for Women), UNDP (United Nations Development Programme), and the British Council. The Ford Foundation played the key role in the 1990s by funding the major women's studies conferences and seminars. In addition to major women's studies projects on reproductive health in China, the Ford Foundation also funded projects on rural women's development, women's education, the mobility of the female population, women's legislation, and the women's and gender study curriculum in higher education. Chinese women's studies receive little domestic funding, and relying on Western and international foundations has been seen as the only option. Together with supplying funding, these foundations have also offered ideas and 'knowledge'. As a Chinese sociologist in the Yunnan Reproductive Health Research Association (YRHRA) explained:

> I can confirm that without the support of the Ford Foundation, the YRHRA would have found it difficult to survive. It is not just the money. The Ford Foundation has supported programmes of reproductive health all over the world and has published guidelines on the programmes. Their support was ideological as well as financial, which is the absolutely important factor for the YRHRA since it was set up.
>
> (interview, Min/Zheng, 1/10/1999)

The second important factor having to do with transnational feminism's entry into China consisted of relationships between Western feminist scholars and Chinese women scholars in the diaspora. Since the beginning of the 1990s, overseas Chinese women's studies scholars have conducted many projects involving women scholars in China. Many have brought with them intellectual resources gathered from their own experiences with feminism while abroad, in addition to contacts with sources of funding (Wang, Z., 1997a). In all of this, the Chinese Society for Women's Studies (CSWS) in the United States is the key organisation for the introduction of gender theory into China. It has also been involved in many co-operative projects with women's studies groups and individuals in China on the subject of gender through conferences, workshops, translations, publications, and training programmes since the beginning of the 1990s (Wang, Z., 1997a; Bao with Xu, 2001; Spakowski, 2001).

In the new wave of travelling transnational feminist theories, the NGO emerged in China as a new form of organisation distinct from the state sector. The NGO-based feminists are focused on doing projects as a novel form of women's and gender practice. These NGOs and the feminists were to play important parts in altering the direction and content of women's and gender studies in China after the 1995 Fourth World Conference on Women.

Women's NGOs in China

There was no tradition of NGOs in China. The concept of non-governmental organisation entered China with the FWCW and the concurrent NGO Forum in 1995. Before this conference, the obvious questions for the Chinese women's movement were "what is an NGO?" and "what is an NGO Forum?" The Chinese Organising Committee had to clarify these matters before it could mobilise Chinese women to participate in the conference. Therefore, an urgent task of the committee was to familiarise itself with the term and develop appropriate mechanisms. In other words, in order to connect with the international track, it was necessary to know where the tracks were and how they were made; and then it must be decided how to connect with them.

'Non-government', a concept that did not exist in the Chinese language, aroused some amusement and confusion. To translate it as *fei-zhengfu* sounded odd in Chinese and made many ask if NGO meant 'anti-government organisation'. Due to this lack of comprehension and recognition of the positive functions of NGOs, it was important to establish a better understanding of the concept in China. According to Liu Bohong:

> At the beginning, the only authoritative interpretation in China came from promotional materials put out by the China Organising Committee, which state that non-governmental organisations cannot be compared to governmental organisations. NGOs are non-profit groups or organisations set up by people who are concerned with particular problems.
>
> (Liu, B., 2001)

The next question was what or who would qualify as an NGO in China? Answering this question was not easy, because there was almost no organisation of women (or men) that could meet the criteria for recognition as an NGO. The answer was arrived at in an unexpected way by the Chinese women's movement at the Asia-Pacific Regional Preparatory Meeting for the NGO Forum held in Manila in November 1993. For the Chinese delegation, which – without any experience with NGOs – was participating for the first time, the NGO meeting was an eye-opening and challenging experience. However, the most surprising thing for the participants was that Huang Qizao, the vice president of ACWF, spoke of women's NGOs in China as actively involved in preparing for the NGO Forum. Her identification of the ACWF as an NGO caused an uproar among participants in the Forum. Although the questions and support from the meeting were controversial, the whole world came to know of the existence of women's NGOs in China. For the Chinese delegation at that meeting, the vision of NGOs and governmental organisations (GOs) as partners rather than as political opponents was a historic incident (Liu, B., 2001).

As a result, the Chinese government formally designated the ACWF "China's largest NGO whose aims are raising the status of women" in the Report of the People's Republic of China on the Implementation of the Nairobi Forward-Looking Strategies for the Advancement of Women (*Zhonghua renmin gongheguo*, 1994: 4; cited from Zhang, N., 2001: 159).

The ACWF has since then used the title of NGO when attending international functions concerning women, but it has not adopted the NGO label for itself in domestic matters. At the 8th National Congress of the ACWF in 1998, the term gender had not been adopted into the congress documents, and the title of NGO was not used with reference to the ACWF. In the end, the ACWF continued to define itself as a 'mass organisation' (*qunzhong tuanti*)[2] and there were no references to the impact of NGOs on the Chinese women's movement in its congress documents (Zhang, N., 2001). Indeed, the designation NGO did not fit the Chinese context, and avoiding the use of this politically sensitive label might have been a survival strategy.

Nonetheless, the concept and practice of using the term NGO did have a visible impact on China and on China's women's movement, where the concept quickly gained popularity among newly founded women's organisations. Even the ACWF came to accept the title of NGO. The ACWF had, after all, been working closely with the UN before and during the women's conference in 1995 when the title was first introduced into China, and it also had a desire to connect with the international track.[3]

From the beginning, most women's NGOs were established in Beijing. These included the Maple Women's Psychological Counselling Centre, the Women's Media Watch Network, the Legal Advice Service Centre, the Centre for Women's Law Studies and Legal Services, Jinglun Family Centre, and *Rural Women Knowing All* magazine.

Another push to set up NGOs came from the field of gender and development. It aimed to facilitate the dissemination of issues related to gender and development to remote rural areas, mainly the southwestern and northwestern regions of China. In contrast to the CCP model, where state-led mass organisations mobilise women from the top down, these newly established women's NGOs functioned as social forces and expanded their networks of horizontal connections, challenging the dominant organisational approach.

The theoretical framework of women's NGOs in China was influenced by the Fourth World Conference on Women. The 1995 Women's Conference was, for instance, a watershed event in terms of drawing attention to the problem of male domestic violence against women in China. When activists in the new NGOs began to address the issue of domestic violence, changes in their way of understanding and reacting to the issue were influenced by their interaction with feminist groups in other parts of the world. Importantly, the very act of openly and publicly addressing domestic violence was legitimised by a conference document (the *Beijing Platform for Action*) in which domestic violence was one of 12 items requiring action on the part of governments. It may have been the issue to receive the most attention by women's NGOs in China after the adoption of the Beijing Platform for Action. As Amrita Basu has correctly pointed out, the campaign against sexual violence was more successful than the efforts to tackle the other issues mentioned in the Beijing Platform for Action,[4] such as the pursuit of women's economic rights (see Bernal and Grewal, 2014). Why did the issue of domestic violence seem to travel more vigorously than others? During these travels, why was the phrase 'violence against women' translated into 'domestic violence' within China? This poses important questions that ought to be resolved.

To return to the research on the issue of women's NGOs, most attention has been paid to the external factors of the term 'NGO travelling to China'. A few scholars have linked this discussion of the external and internal factors together in an attempt to understand the phenomenon of the NGO as it emerged in the context of China amid the economic and social transformations of the 1990s. Although some authors noticed that the NGO would influence the most dynamic forms of social organisation within the market economy which demand efficiency, they thought that the NGO would replace the system of the work unit (*danwei*) and fill the spaces from which the state and government had withdrawn in the declining social system (Liu, B., 2001: 145).

A positive picture was drawn in which the non-governmental or community-based organisation would be a catalyst for building civil society in China. Scholars and activists of women's and gender studies envisioned civil society as a public space between citizens and the state, including voluntary associations, social movements, religious groups, and the media. For the Chinese government, however, the growth of civil society might offer very different possibilities. As Xu Feng suggests, "The Global civil society is articulated to the Chinese

State in achieving the State's goal of off-loading social responsibilities to society itself" (Xu, 2009). Perhaps what we see in the making is civil society, neoliberal style. The dissimilar objectives for expanding civil society, and the uncertain political situation in China, have put NGOs in a difficult situation where they have to make the best of it on their own.

How far would the gender-related NGOs be prepared to go to fulfil these aspirations? We can gain an idea of this by scrutinising one of the important activities of NGOs in China: doing projects.

'Doing projects'

In July 1997 I returned to China to take part in a workshop on Chinese Women and Development which was to be held in Nanjing. One of the significant phrases heard during that trip was 'doing projects'. Almost every women's studies scholar I met had been involved in some project (combining research and action) and had been given funding from foreign foundations to do these projects. To me, this was a very new phenomenon, because Chinese women's studies scholars and activists during the 1980s were preoccupied with teaching and writing and had no such funding. I was wondering what doing projects meant and what would it mean for women's studies in China. Why and how had this movement materialised?

The political and financial pressures following the events of Tiananmen Square in 1989 resulted in a shift in Chinese women's studies, from theoretical research to practical activities. There followed a considerable growth in the contact with transnational feminism and international agencies during the 1990s. With this new flow of transnational feminist ideas into China during the 1990s, how best to connect to the theories and research methods of the world at large became an important issue for Chinese women's studies scholars. The issues of globalisation and localisation had already been of growing concern to women's and gender studies scholars for a number of years. At the "Women's Studies in China" NGO Forum associated with the FWCW, the attention paid to the concepts internationalisation, globalisation, and localisation by Chinese women's studies scholars was a part of the endeavour to connect with the international track of the women's movements around the world (Women's Studies Institute, 1995). Transnational feminism had travelled to China, but this time via the UN.

This situation can be explored further by examining a number of articles by Liu Bohong, who was one of the major scholars from ACWF working on 'gender mainstreaming'.[5] In an article from 1996, Liu argued that information exchange between China and abroad had increased because the FWCW had taken place in Beijing. In 1995, Liu continued, the interests of Chinese women's studies had developed to include women's rights, women and the media, women's oral history, and studies on minority women. In addition, research had probed the most pressing problems faced by Chinese women, in particular in relation to the '12 domains referred to in the *Platform for Action* and adopted by the UN Fourth World Conference on Women. Liu also noted a new trend: Chinese women's studies was following the interests of the international community. This, she argued, would enable Chinese women to gain knowledge about feminist ideas and women's movements from abroad and to develop a voice in the international community. On the other hand, the issues addressed by the international community were not necessarily the same as the interests of Chinese women. Therefore, the answer to the question of what Chinese women's studies should do was to rely on itself.

In an article of 1999, Liu Bohong made the point that the influence of the FWCW and the *Platform for Action* on Chinese women's and gender studies had been considerable, and that the theory of gender as a category of analysis had been accepted by Chinese women's studies. Liu also noted a new trend of joint activities on the part of women's studies and development studies. She pointed out that women's and development studies were new and important fields for Chinese women's studies, not least because China was undergoing a significant social transition. In accordance with the views of the UN on gender mainstreaming, Liu emphasised that women's studies should influence mainstream policy-making. This had not only been a distinguishing feature of Chinese women's studies since the 1980s, it was also an important step towards carrying out the resolutions of the FWCW (Liu, B., 1999). In contrast with her 1996 article, Liu's article of 1999 stressed the importance of translating gender and development from the FWCW to the Chinese mainstream.

What did women's studies scholars and activists think of doing projects? For the newly developed NGOs, the first important task was to reconsider the position and functions of the organisations themselves. Gao Xiaoxian, the director of the Shangxi Research Association for Women and Family in Shaanxi province, has conducted many research projects on women and development since the early 1990s. Her experience reflects this process:

> I was considering the relationship of research to action when we set up the Association in 1986, and we wanted to do research, not do a project with research added on. Changing from 'doing research' to 'doing projects' involved the influence of funding, because the donors prefer you to 'do projects'. However, I have realised that the aim of research should be to change the situation of women. There are so many women's problems in China. As researchers, it seems that we may be separating ourselves from the mass of women if we turn a blind eye to women's problems. In the meantime, considered from the angle of women's organisations, the advantage of these action projects is that they encourage the government to

recognise the NGOs. When you have done something for public welfare, you will be noticed by the government. So I think it will be of benefit to push the work of NGOs in China.

(interview, Min/Gao, 14/7/1999)

For scholars in academic circles, looking for new research themes with links to funding was perhaps the sole way to carry on doing women's and gender studies. Du Fangqin suggested that

> the majority of women's studies centres in China operated under 'four shortages' (*si wu*) i.e. no regular staff, no funding, no facilities, and no time. Half of the women's studies centres existed in name only because they had no 'project' (*keti*) and no funding.
>
> (Du, 2001)

In order to survive under these circumstances, the scholars involved in women's studies had to adopt new themes, ideas, and strategies. For example, on her trip to the United States in 1992, Du Fangqin recognised that

> I gradually became aware of the mainstream in the world's women's movement . . . Three UN conferences on women had been held already, but we didn't know that 'Equality, Development and Peace' were the aims of the women's movements until 20 years after they had been set. That was why I connected the themes on 'development' and 'health' with Chinese women for the seminar in 1993.
>
> (Du, 1997: 143)

On her trip to the United States, Du not only encountered new themes, she also met her new partner, the CSWS. Back home, Du and the CSWS decided to organise a workshop in 1993 on the theme of "Chinese Women and Development – Status, Health, and Employment". In this workshop, the term gender was formally introduced into women's studies circles in China for the first time.

Doing projects has been a learning experience for many Chinese women's studies scholars and activists since the 1990s. Together with these women's studies scholars and activists, Gao Xiaoxian had to learn how to carry out projects as required, step by step. Gao explained:

> For instance, I visited many women's law centres in Manila in 1993, and it made me think that law is an important part of sorting out women's problems. When I came back home to China, the Women's Federation in our province asked our institute to be involved in drafting women's law. It was a very good opportunity, but I didn't know how to deal with it, because my subject was not law. However, at the workshop on 'Chinese Women and

Development' in Tianjin in 1993 I had met a law Professor Tan Jingchang, who came from America. She suggested to me that I should apply for funding and do this as a project. It was the first time that I learned to write a proposal and to apply for funding.

(interview, Min/Gao, 14/7/1999)

For women's studies scholars and activists involved in action research with poor women, the issue of methodology was bound to emerge sooner or later. Gao Xiaoxian was one of the scholars who thought about this issue in great detail:

In 1992, I studied feminist courses in Australia, and I believe that feminist research has its own character. For instance, using gender theory to analyse issues, paying attention to the relationship between researchers and research using qualitative methods, all of these have a strong appeal to me. I did not know why but I felt very easy in accepting them. Perhaps this is due to the fact that I have a lot of experience in research on rural women. . . . I think the best way is to connect with these research methods. Chinese women's studies addressed the issue of jiegui at the FWCW, but we found it difficult to understand each other when we tried to communicate. Of course, there is a problem of language, but more than that there is the problem of research methods. Many Western people think that there are many vague and general opinions in Chinese research. . . . I was told that most research published abroad on Chinese women had been done by Western scholars, so I have a strong feeling about making Chinese women's studies go out to the world. But how? If we don't pay attention to the study of methodology, we will be unable to do this and unable to enter into dialogue with the rest of the world.

(interview, Min/Gao, 14/7/1999)

In contrast with women's studies in the 1980s, the new trend of women's and gender studies had to deal with social issues, which are more closely linked with subjects such as sociology and anthropology than with literature and history. For some women's studies scholars and activists, the lack of training in social science research made doing projects a difficult way of conducting feminist research. In the process, as Du Fangqin experienced, many copied methods, concepts, and terms from transnational feminisms without adequate knowledge of how to employ them. On this topic, Du described a project on rural women and development she had conducted in Ding Xian County:

We invited a group of women's studies scholars to help us design the research framework. At that time, Gao Xiaoxian had just come back from Australia and brought with her ideas on feminist research methods. She introduced us to quantitative research methods and a lot of new concepts but we didn't understand what they meant! A scholar, Li Dun, suggested that we should adopt the methods of traditional anthropology, but he couldn't figure out how to use these methods for researching our own culture. In the end, these scholars said to me, 'Your subject is involved in the study of history, so why don't you do something on the historical and cultural situation of rural women?' In order to find some way to do the project we explored the methods of interview, document studies, and qualitative research again and again. We had neither the expertise nor training in these research methods. In the end, we had to design our research project according to the methods of historical studies.

(interview, Min/Du, 7/4/1999)

By this time, Du and other members of the Centre for Women's Studies at Tianjin Normal University had the opportunity of being trained by Oxfam to carry out an oral history project. In the end, they decided to adopt this method in their Ding Xian County project. She set out the reasons:

We were focusing on the method of oral history in our projects, and adding some development theory. I noticed that Gail Hershatter (an American scholar who carried out several research projects on Chinese women) used the oral history method in her later research project in Shaanxi. She applied categories, such as body, work, public, and private. I tried to add these categories to our projects. . . . We didn't know about the idea of 'difference' until American scholars addressed it. No matter what its meaning, it is useful to explain the different identities of women in China. It confirms for us that we should look at the issue of difference, even among rural women. I am adding the idea into my research with consideration of the differences among women in a village, because of their different economic situations and also that of giving birth to children of different sexes. Another idea I have learned is the concept of 'experience'. Everybody knows this word, but as a philosophical concept it is very new and very rich for Chinese women's studies scholars. We should pay more attention to it.

(interview, Min/Du, 7/4/1999)

For most women's studies groups, *jiegui* means connecting with the international track, learning new ideas and new methods. Since the early 1990s, Chinese women's studies has gradually been reshaped towards doing projects. During this process, the impact of global feminism and foreign foundations has been considerable, and these have become another force shaping public discourse on women and women's studies in China. Certainly, women's studies everywhere in the world has always lacked resources. In my experience, having been involved in teaching and research, there was no funding at all for women's studies in the 1980s, but we managed without and developed research in a distinctive way. However, as China moved towards a marketisation of the economy during the 1990s, the situation changed significantly. On the one hand, the government did not contribute enough money to develop subjects within the social sciences and humanities, and there was certainly no financial support from government for women's studies in higher education (Du, 2001). On the other hand, foreign foundations, such as the Ford Foundation, did start to provide funding for women's studies. With the emerging market came further expansion. Forming new contacts, linkages, and networks with international funding agencies and international NGOs – and carrying out projects funded by Western foundations based on priorities specified by these funding agencies – came to be seen as the only way to survive for women's and gender studies in China.

The funding organisations were interested in supporting the work of Chinese women's studies, primarily on issues which were addressed in the 1995 FWCW documents, such as women and poverty, women and health, and violence against women. Not surprisingly, for Chinese women's studies there was in many cases no choice but to engage with a given project in the manner required by the funders.

The Chinese historian Du Fangqin, whom I quoted previously, has organised many projects funded by the Ford Foundation since the 1990s. Du provides a typical example of funding dependency:

> When we were doing projects with rural women and development during the 1990s, we tried to make these as close as possible to the subjects of history and anthropology, although we did not do this very well. There is a whole area of theory and methods of academic research in the West, whereas we are in the 'Third World' and are pressed for time to catch up, so we were compelled to do the projects.
>
> (interview, Min/Du, 7/4/1999)

With the idea of catching up with the international community – that is to say, the West – Chinese women's studies, like many of our Third World and Second World counterparts, had to give up our own traditions and follow the international trend. Feminist ideas travelled from UN sources and from global locations, primarily from UN-based transnational feminism. During this time, translation as knowledge production broadly referred to an approach to social transformation with regard to gender issues through a project-based global agenda, but most of the Chinese women's studies scholars and activists I interviewed or whose work I read remained silent on the issue of this intellectual 'post-colonisation'. They did not question what the term international community meant any more than they questioned where global feminism came from. One claim was that "gender theory should not be regarded as merely Western, as it was proposed by the UN that it is global" (Liu and Wu, 2000: 48). Stressing its global roots might make it more acceptable or empowering for women's studies in China, but might it not also hide the hegemony of global feminism and the real power relationship between global and local feminisms?

There were different views on this issue in China, but the real question was who controlled the direction of women's studies research in China from the middle of the 1990s, when Chinese women's studies started relying on foreign foundations. Li Xiaojiang, one of the pioneers of women's studies in China, objected to doing projects, pointing out that doing projects involved being post-colonial as a result of being dependent on external financial support and networks:

> 'Doing projects' is another name for 'research on women and development'. No one is willing to do research on 'women's literature', 'women's theory', because no one is offering money for these kinds of projects.
> (interview, Min/Li, X., 3/3/1999)

Li's point of view was not surprising. In the field of women's studies, 'theorising theory on women', which had been an important part of Chinese women's studies since the 1980s, almost ceased in the 1990s. The interruption of the theoretical debate was inevitable in women's studies during the 1990s in China.

My concern was that doing projects might affect the research direction of Chinese women's studies scholars. On the one hand, it might lead them to take a deeper view of how to handle local rural women's questions and to construct a critical discourse on reproductive health. On the other hand, as the scholars I spoke with in Yunnan kept reminding me, the foreign foundations and international organisations constantly introduced new projects into Yunnan, leaving researchers continually involved in doing projects, which had them travelling between several field projects and leaving them no time to do theoretical work. These projects, which were required by global institutions and donors, were usually managed on the basis of results. My interviewees indicated that when they worked on such projects, they became dominated by issues of accountability and results-based management, and the possibilities for long-term feminist alternatives thus dried up. As Zhao Jie, one of the major scholars of gender and development in China, told me, her main academic interest was concerned with feminist theory and feminist sociology, but her involvement in doing projects meant that she was too busy on several of these to pay much attention to her own research interests (interview, Min/Zhao, J., 30/3/1999).

After a decade, when the scholars rethought the journey of doing projects, or more broadly the history of the project "Gender and Development" (GAD) in China, a critical voice emerged:

> The term GAD actually refers only to a strategy and methods, rather than to the ultimate goal of achieving social, including gender, equality and justice. In China at present, although gender equality is guaranteed in national law and policy, in terms of both scope and depth, the work being done to promote gender equality remains marginal.
>
> (Zhao, 2011: 186–187)

When I dwelt on the thoughts that I had concerning the travelling of feminist ideas to women's studies in China during the 1980s and the 1990s, I eventually concluded that there was something different about the routes taken by transnational feminist ideas during this time. During my fieldwork in 1999, I explored this question with Li Huiying, one of the key figures involved in introducing a gender perspective into women's studies in the 1990s:

LI: Why was it so difficult to introduce feminist ideas into China in the 1980s but not in the 1990s? It was due to the different routes involved. At that time (the 1980s) feminism was introduced by intellectuals in academic circles. This time (the 1990s) feminism came to China via the FWCW and government officials. China is a member of the UN and the host of the 1995 FWCW, so the government had to undertake the resolutions of the UN.

MIN: You mean feminism came into China through the mainstream in the 1990s?

LI: Yes.

MIN: So, you are saying that during the 1980s, feminism travelled to China in a heterodox or a non-mainstream way?

LI: Yes! That is what I would say.

(interview, Min/Li, H., 3/3/1999)

As Li makes clear, the wave of Chinese women's studies and feminism in the 1990s was quite different from that of the 1980s. If the trend of women's studies in the 1980s was dominated by Chinese scholars and activists, in the 1990s there was a shift towards what was occurring in the global context. The new wave of Chinese women's studies during the 1990s cannot be seen as an isolated or local development; it was, rather, part of the global pattern. In the 1990s, the diversity of *jiegui* replaced the discourse of enlightenment, while doing projects replaced the philosophical explorations of theorising theory on women in Chinese women's studies.

Jiegui was based on the view that China had for some time been outside the international community and that on its return, it had to change its gauge to fit the international track – the track of globalisation. Indeed, globalisation, beyond being an economic process involving the development of global financial and capital markets, is a political process that "has involved the restructuring of the political environment, re-positioning the nation-state in a web of trans-national networks and institutions" (Walby, 2002: 551). In China, the major event of the process of *jiegui* and globalisation for Chinese women came with China hosting the 1995 FWCW. This process, as Zhang Naihua pointed out,

> not only made the government reaffirm its ideological commitment to gender equality, it also helped 'internationalize' women's issues, forcing China to adhere to UN documents and facilitating China's connection with the international women's movement. As a result, Chinese women's groups have become the only social groups in China that have such broad, direct connections with their counterparts in foreign countries.
> (Zhang, N., 2001: 175–176)

Chinese feminist scholars, activists, and the ACWF all embraced the 1995 FWCW and the concomitant translations of feminism as aspects of this new political environment. China saw two translations of feminism in the 1990s. One was from the top (the UN's World Health Organisation) and another was from the West, mainly from the United States. But this time, the translation of the UN tracks exerted dominant power. The translations of the 1995 FWCW, from organisations (NGOs) to documents (the *Platform for Action* and the *Beijing Declaration*) had permitted great visibility of women's issues both internationally and in China. So much happened, and so quickly, in the name of *jiegui*. A new kind of organisation, the NGO, emerged as an entity distinct from the state sector. The ideas of gender and gender and development were given priority in Chinese women's studies circles, not only because the FWCW put these issues on the agenda of the UN via recurrent conferences and NGO Forums, but also because of financial support from international and in particular Western foundations.

The ACWF, with its close links with and subordination to the CCP, had to respond to the contradictory impact of reforms on women, the changing needs and demands of a much more diverse constituency of women, and the emergence of new women's groups. In doing so, it came under increasing official pressure not only to prioritise the interests of the party, but also to attend to the needs of women. Therefore, the ACWF needed to adopt a positive attitude towards *jiegui*. For the ACWF, both the preparations for the 1995 FWCW and the actual event itself provided an opportunity to discover some of the dominant themes in global gender discourse, as well as to gain organisational prestige and experience of working with women's NGOs. International projects, funding, and discourses were introduced to the ACWF. In the changing context of transnational feminism in China, the ACWF had to play a dual role, as political assistant of the Communist Party and representative of women's interests (Jin, 2001).

One of the significant developments in Chinese society in the past two decades has been the development of NGOs and discussions regarding civil society. We are aware that civil society needs space separate from government action and should provide for frequent and intense exchange among individuals, groups, and organisations with political vision. The question is what civil society in today's fast-changing China actually *is*. Or, to put it another way, what is meant by a civil society in the context of China? How are women's NGOs to build this civil society? These questions have not been fully discussed in the field of women's and gender studies. Without interrogating the bigger picture of civil society both globally and locally, I fear that NGOs will be unable to travel very far in China.

My concern with doing projects is that this shift has affected the direction of research in women's and gender studies. In order to achieve *jiegui* in the short term, Chinese women's studies had to copy and mimic Western and transnational feminist themes, concepts, and terms. The result has been that people involved in women's and gender studies have used feminist theories and discourses that have their basis elsewhere in the world. These feminisms do not include the experiences of Chinese women. Perhaps this is an unavoidable stage in the process of developing a new subject. However, it seems to me that sooner or later, Chinese women's studies scholars and activists will find that copying these themes, terms, and methods is no replacement for creating their own.

The ACWF and women's studies scholars and activists employed the idea of *jiegui* to challenge existing internal hegemonies, and to assert that global and Western feminist ideas represented advanced, progressive thought. In the meantime, this may have blocked inquiry into who and what represented the global and what constituted the international community. It also seems to have delayed an exploration of the limits of global feminism and prevented critical analysis of just which Western feminisms travelled and why.

In the next chapter, I shall look more closely at how transnational feminism and women's and gender studies travelled through China with one of the earliest Chinese NGOs, the Yunnan Reproductive Health Research Association (YRHRA). I will also examine the role of the CSWS, the US-based feminist organisation which constitutes a traveller group.

Notes

1   With the new flow of gender studies into China, the term women's studies gradually changed to gender studies from around the mid-1990s. At times, the two terms have been put together as women's/gender studies.
2   A mass organisation means, in theory, a party-state organisation. Its funding, policies, and leadership are determined by the government, but while its functions and purposes are

the same as those of other government bodies, it has less status and authority than other government bodies.
3   For further research and discussion on this topic, see Hsiung and Wong (1998); Liu, B. (2001); Zhang (2001); Milwertz and Bu (2007); Liu, Hu, and Liao (2009); Xu (2009); Wang and Zhang (2010); and Li, S. (2014).
4   The 12 domains are: women and poverty, education and training of women, women and health, violence against women, women and armed conflict, women and the economy, women in power and decision-making, institutional mechanisms for the advancement of women, human rights of women, women and the media, women and the environment, and the girl-child.
5   Liu has written three articles on this topic. See Liu, Bohong (1995), "Trends in Women's Studies in China in 1994", *Collection of Women's Studies*, 1, pp. 9–11; Liu, Bohong (1996), "When Everybody Adds the Fuel the Flames Rise High", *Collection of Women's Studies*, 1, pp. 14–19; Liu, Bohong (1999), "The Fourth World Conference on Women and Women's Studies in China", *Women's Studies, Reprinted Materials from the Press*, 2, pp. 46–51.

5 The cases of two NGOs

In this chapter, I will examine two key non-governmental organisations (NGOs) which were, in my opinion, two of the most important players in the 'contact zone' from the middle of the 1990s to the early 2000s. These two NGOs, the Chinese Society for Women's Studies (CSWS) and the Yunnan Reproductive Health Research Association (YRHRA), make excellent cases for exploring the practice of transnational feminisms in China, especially as it relates to gender and development. These two organisations each had their own approach to circulating and translating gender theories and practices. While the CSWS acted as a traveller from outside China, the YRHRA functioned as a key local NGO inside China.

The Chinese Society for Women's Studies (CSWS)

The CSWS is a US-based feminist organisation, constituting what I refer to as a traveller group. The CSWS was formed in 1989, when seven Chinese female students in various disciplines (history, sociology, comparative literature, and American studies) gathered to share their experiences with scholars and activists of women's studies at the annual conference of Chinese historians held in the United States. Through the 1990s, the CSWS had a membership of more than 100 feminist scholars and activists living and working in the United States, Canada, Europe, and China.

From the outset, the goals of the society were clear: to promote the study of Chinese women in the international academic community, to develop scholarly exchanges between women in China and their counterparts in other parts of the world, and to collaborate with feminist scholars and activists in China in order to promote women's studies in China. In order to achieve these goals, the CSWS undertook a series of collaborative projects in China and the United States, building up a transnational network for communication on issues of concern to Chinese women. In considering the flow of feminist ideas and theories into China, the CSWS cannot be ignored.

From its inception, many overseas members of the society, particularly those who had moved away from China from the mid-1980s and who had been actively involved in women's studies before leaving, had strong ties with feminist scholars and activists in China. One of these was Xu Wu, the former co-director of the CSWS and a former colleague of Du Fangqin's and mine. (Du Fangqin was the major organiser of collaborative projects co-sponsored by the CSWS and Tianjin Normal University in China.) Before Xu Wu moved to the United States, we had worked together to promote women's studies at Tianjin Normal University in the 1980s.

During the 1990s, the CSWS organised many projects to promote Chinese women's studies. I shall outline three of these collaborative projects on women and development, not only because these were the major projects conducted by CSWS members with their counterparts in China, but also because doing these collaborative projects in Tianjin, Nanjing, and Chengdu involved a process which moved from being misunderstood, to negotiation, to reaching an understanding between the CSWS and its counterparts in China. Each project included meetings and workshops, conducting research, translating English articles into Chinese, writing articles and reports, and publishing books.[1]

The first collaborative CSWS project began in 1992, when a conference on "Engendering China: Women, Culture, and the State" was hosted by Harvard University and Wellesley College in the United States. Wanting to promote women's studies in China, several members of the CSWS and Du Fangqin from Tianjin Normal University approached Mary Ann Burris, who was then the Ford Foundation Program Officer in Beijing, about funding possibilities and, at the same time, engaged in intensive discussions to explore ways of pursuing a collaborative project in China. With encouragement from Burris, feminist scholars on both sides of the Pacific began to work out a fundraising proposal and organised the first workshop on "Chinese Women and Development" in 1993 in Tianjin, co-sponsored by the CSWS and Tianjin Normal University (Bao with Xu, 2001).

At this workshop, scholars from China presented their research and CSWS members discussed the concept of gender in relation to various aspects of life, ranging from the labour market and health to demographic studies and development theories. During the workshop, gender perspectives introduced by members of the CSWS became the focus of discussion. Many participants found the concept of gender useful and enlightening and expressed a strong desire to learn about feminist theories and methodology more systematically. More exchanges and research collaboration between scholars inside and outside of China were planned and subsequently carried out (Zhang with Xu, 1995).

Following the success of the first workshop, the CSWS and the Jiangsu Academy of Social Sciences (JASS) jointly organised a second workshop in 1997, this time on "Women and Development in China", held in Nanjing (the capital of Jiangsu province). Over 100 people attended this workshop, including 15 Chinese scholars from overseas along with international scholars from Hong

Kong, the UK, the Netherlands, Canada, and the United States. I was one of the Chinese scholars, and I returned from a position as a visiting scholar in the UK in order to participate.

Perhaps due to the success of the 1993 workshop, the same model was chosen for the Nanjing workshop: CSWS members introduced women's and gender studies and development studies from the West, while Chinese scholars and activists presented their own research. Although the overseas scholars wanted to open up new topics and discuss recent items of more relevance in the Chinese context, the lack of both first-hand experience of women's and gender studies in China and of communication with their Chinese counterparts meant that Chinese perspectives and practices were not treated as the focal point for this workshop, leaving part of the audience frustrated and disappointed.

What had changed between the 1993 workshop and this one was that in 1997, the majority of participants from China had a strong interest in presentations emphasising action research and research with policy implications, such as a project on micro-banking or small loans for poor rural women. Other hot topics involved women and poverty, unemployed urban women, women's health and reproductive health, and women and mass media. Researchers and project workers wanted more methodological information on needs assessments, programme planning, and analysing data (Xu, 1997). In order to satisfy these participants, the workshop organisers had to add an evening training session on sociological research methods.

A preparatory committee for the third workshop on "Women and Development in China", to be held in 1999, was organised during the Nanjing workshop. Scholars who were interested in promoting women's and gender studies programmes in higher education organised a separate meeting. It seemed at the time that women's and gender studies would fracture into two parts: one concentrating on women in poor rural areas (the field of women/gender and development), and the other focusing on women's and gender studies programmes in higher education (the field of women's and gender studies).[2]

I had been absent from China for five years when the 1997 workshop was held, and I experienced complicated feelings as the event came under way. Although I was 'at home' in China and shared a lot of ideas with my friends in Chinese women's studies, women's studies in China had, nevertheless, changed a great deal and this home had become an unfamiliar place. Doing projects had become the dominant framework for doing research in Chinese women's studies, and funding had become crucial for researchers. At the same time, I felt uncomfortable with the hierarchical setup of the workshop, with overseas scholars teaching domestic scholars and activists about feminism in a particular way and developing a particular model for doing research. Certainly, some scholars in the CSWS had also noticed that the organisation had attained an advantageous position. Due to the lack of formal nationwide women's studies organisations in China, the CSWS has become a connecting point, bringing scholars and activists from different regions and sectors together. In addition, scholars in China wanted the CSWS to continue in its role as grant applicant and co-ordinator for women and development projects in China. In other words, the CSWS was in an extremely powerful position.

Aware of the uneven relations of power, the CSWS made a number of changes as they prepared for the third workshop on "Women and Development". As some members of the CSWS pointed out:

> From the CSWS' previous applications for developmental project funding, one can find that the frequently-used terms were 'introduce', 'training', and 'education'. In the 1998 Chengdu workshop proposal, those words were replaced by the concepts of 'participatory', 'empowerment', and 'facilitation'.
> (Xu, Ma, and Li, 2000: 5)

This time, the planning committee in the CSWS tried to change its position from being an expert to being an equal partner with its sisters at home. The CSWS was thereby responding to several challenges.

The first challenge came from the CSWS's Chinese minority members and indigenous women groups. One CSWS member, Wu Ga of the Yi ethnic group, asked Han women scholars if their 'Chinese women's studies' were actually 'Han women's studies' (Han is the largest ethnic group in China). In 1997, both before and after the Nanjing workshop, the role of the CSWS 'trainers' (or international experts) was questioned by some CSWS members, and also by their collaborators in China and the Ford Foundation.

The second challenge related to the practical needs of indigenous women's studies scholars. Before the Chengdu workshop, the planning committee of the CSWS received requests for participatory rural appraisal (PRA) training. Joint participation in action research in women's studies and in gender and development (GAD) in China had been very effective, and therefore the committee decided to apply PRA principles to the workshop: equity among participants, learning from each other, and empowerment for all.

The third challenge came from the need for networking. The concept of participation was questioned within the planning committee: "Participation for what? Who should empower whom, and for what? We also put the concept into the specific context: what was the reason for us to use this new approach to organise the workshop?" (Xu, Ma, and Li, 2000: 6). The answer was that a feminist participatory approach would promote networking among participants from diverse backgrounds, such as people from women's studies, Gender and Development Program personnel, women's federation officials, and village women. The organisers emphasised that overseas participants should learn from indigenous people.

The CSWS responded positively to these challenges. Bao Xiaolan, one of the key members of the CSWS, writes that "the third CSWS collaborative project was the society's first attempt to extend its network beyond scholarly circles in China. It turned out to be the greatest challenge we had ever encountered" (Bao with Xu 2001: 85). The process of finding a host for the project in China was not smooth sailing, and eventually Sichuan was chosen, not only because it was one of the major provinces in southwest China, but also because it had not been significantly influenced by any of the major feminist projects around the country. Furthermore, the planning committee found the leadership of the Sichuan Women's Federation to be very supportive.

The "Gender, Poverty, and Rural Development Participatory Workshop" was finally held in Chengdu, Sichuan, in December 1998. It brought together people from four areas of research and activists: Chinese scholars of women's studies at home and abroad; researchers and practitioners in development projects in China; members of the Women's Federation at various levels; and a number of grass-roots women activists from various ethnic groups and areas in Sichuan. In contrast to the conventional way of holding conferences in China, where presentations by scholars and officials would occupy the centre of attention, the Chengdu workshop featured discussion and promoted the equal exchange of ideas among all participants. Everyone was encouraged to take the initiative in questioning each other's perceptions and identifying new issues in relation to poverty from gender and ethnic perspectives. This new approach generated enormous enthusiasm among participants in the workshop. Many participants began to question the state's definitions of 'poverty' and a 'poor household', and the approaches adopted by many poverty alleviation programmes in China, including those nominally aimed at assisting women but which in fact targeted poverty as an issue (Bao with Xu, 2001).

Perhaps the biggest achievement of the Chengdu workshop was the networking and communication between the four types of participants and the establishment of a series of workshops and research projects on gender and development (Xu, Ma, and Li, 2000). For years, dialogue between feminist insiders and outsiders had been described thus: "Everyone uses her own terminology and talks to herself" (Gao Xiaoxian, cited from Xu, Ma, and Li, 2000: 7). At the Chengdu workshop, however, the communication gap between the different groups narrowed considerably.

Almost all participants at the workshop felt they learned a great deal from interacting with people from social groups other than their own and were, in one way or another, empowered by their participation. Many feminist scholars began to question their previous views about women's lives in China and emphasised the need to develop a new research approach to encompass the diverse experiences of women of different social and ethnic groups. Many participants were impressed by the democratic atmosphere of the workshop and began to question institutional inequality. As one of the cadres of a local Women's Federation chapter pointed out:

> This is the first meeting that led me to understand the true meaning of 'grass-roots participation'. I have worked in the Women's Federation for more than ten years and have attended numerous meetings. All that I have learned is how to listen to the leaders when they talk, and how to not talk unless my superiors assign me to talk. This workshop is indeed an eye-opening experience for me. Now I see what equal rights for everyone in a society can mean.
>
> (Bao with Xu, 2001: 89)

The CSWS members who attended the Chengdu workshop shared many responses similar to those of the other participants. However, as overseas Chinese, they had their own reactions. In their personal reflections on the workshop, they called it a homecoming, and one said, "I found my roots and felt at home". As overseas Chinese, they felt they had been marginalised by both their home culture and their transplanted culture. They felt that they belonged to neither and were left in-between. At the workshop, however, they, like all the other participants, felt welcomed and needed, and that they had both something to offer and many things to learn (Xu et al., 1999). As a traveller group, this time the CSWS worked as an equal counterpart with the local grass-roots NGOs and the Women's Federation.

With these three collaborative projects, the role of the CSWS changed from introductory training to participatory empowerment. The work was still part of connecting with the international track, but instead of concentrating on the flow of globalising feminism into China, the focus after the Chengdu workshop in 1998 was on connecting with the local track through dialogue between diverse groups of women. The most important factor here was the change to sharing feminist participatory principles with local partners. Based on these principles, the CSWS planning committee fully respected the local host's role in setting up the workshop programme and inviting grass-roots women to the workshop. Local women's autonomy and ownership of the workshop evolved as driving forces to ensure a successful project.

To understand the changes occurring in the CSWS during the 1990s, it is important to note Bao Xiaolan and Xu Wu's explanation:

> Like most of our cohort who received training in Women's Studies during the late 1980s and early 1990s, we had been influenced by the 'theory of difference', which emphasizes the importance of recognising the diverse experiences of women in feminist interactions.
>
> (Bao with Xu, 2001: 91)

Experiencing feminist practice in China made some members of CSWS realise the importance of the theory of difference. They claimed that without recognising the importance of understanding women's diverse experiences, they could not have organised a workshop like the one in Chengdu. It was the awareness of the unequal power relations in feminist interactions and the political importance of the location that led them to re-examine the relationship with their partners in China and create an intersubjective 'contact zone' at the Chengdu workshop for all participants (Bao with Xu, 2001).

Bao and Xu, however, describe only a part of the group's philosophy here. Another part had to do with forging alliances between groups who were differently positioned:

> In many cases this will involve a hard political struggle of uniting women who are themselves divided by their class position or their ethnicity around a common series of issues, as well as working with other groups of oppressed peoples. In different circumstances, we need to ask ourselves not only what our differences are but also what are our commonalities.
> (McDowell, 1996: 42–43)

The CSWS should, as a US-based feminist organisation involved with projects of travelling theory, have been more aware of how the distribution of power might interact with the production of knowledge. Mignolo says:

> Knowledge production is not detached from the sensibilities of geohistorical location and that historical locations, in the modern/colonial world, have been shaped by the coloniality of power. Scholarship, travelling theories, wandering and sedentary scholars in the First or the Third World, cannot avoid the marks in their bodies imprinted by the coloniality of power, which, in the last analysis, orient their thinking.
> (Mignolo, 2000: 185–186)

In China, research projects had since the early 1990s been executed as collaborations between teams from the CSWS and women's studies scholars in China, but the power relationship involved in the process of knowledge production was not revealed until the latter part of the 1990s.

The Yunnan Reproductive Health Research Association (YRHRA)

The first time I heard of the Yunnan Reproductive Health Research Association (YRHRA) was in 1997 at the Nanjing Workshop on Women and Development. Zhang Kaining, a professor at Kunming Medical College and founder and director of the YRHRA, presented a paper at the Nanjing workshop introducing his organisation, which was the first NGO to deal with issues of reproductive health in China. What surprised me was that as a male professor, Zhang referred to feminist research on women's health several times at the workshop. Engaging in feminist research on women's health was very rare in the Chinese academy in the 1990s, especially among male scholars. Therefore, I was curious about why the YRHRA had been set up in Yunnan, a poor and remote province of China, and also why Zhang Kaining had preferred to focus on feminist research. I also wondered how the YRHRA was adapting feminist research to its local context.

With these questions in mind, I decided that the YRHRA should become one of my PhD research topics. At the end of the workshop, I talked with Zhang Kaining about my research. As a result, I received an invitation to go to Kunming to carry out fieldwork, and he also gave me two books on reproductive health written by members of the YRHRA. In March 1999, I went to Kunming to visit the YRHRA and interview Professor Zhang and his colleagues.

In the late 1990s, journeying by train from Beijing to Kunming took two days and two nights, and the trip made it very clear why Yunnan was referred to as a 'remote frontier'. Yunnan Province shares borders with Burma, Laos, and Vietnam. Its distance from Beijing and its rugged mountainous terrain have historically kept Yunnan a frontier state, a perception reinforced by the province's large non-Han Chinese population. More than one-third of the province's 38 million people belong to one of 52 ethnic minority groups (of the 55 ethnic minority groups in China, 52 can be found in Yunnan). Yunnan is also one of the poorest provinces in China, with an annual per capita income (in 1991) of just over 1,000 yuan (US$178.57) (Yunnan Provincial Bureau of Statistics, 1992, cited from Li, V. et al., 1998).

Yet, Yunnan's economic underdevelopment and potential natural advantages have attracted the attention of a wide array of global development organisations. During the 1990s, a significant number of NGOs appeared and came to play increasingly important roles in some areas of China, especially in the sphere of the women's and gender studies movement.[3] For instance, over 200 NGOs set up their offices in Kunming, the capital of Yunnan Province, thus exceeding the number of offices set up in Beijing (Chen, 2007). With international projects flowing into Yunnan after the 1990s, a number of scholars and activists became involved in projects on women/gender and development. Gradually, the Women's Federation in Yunnan also became involved in many projects that were supported by international NGOs. These institutions have become tangible outlets for services for poor people, minority groups, and women. Among the positive results is that according to one index of women's political participation, it ranks fourth (Ma and Jia, 2008), and the country has also seen the development of a network of scholars, activists, NGOs, and government agencies.[4]

Professor Zhang was my first interviewee in Kunming. His story started in 1989. From 1989 to 1992, Zhang was a visiting scholar at Leeds University and then at Cambridge University. He told me:

> My aim was very simple at that time. I hoped to find a new research direction for my teaching and for the public health research section at Kunming Medical College, because I was the Director of that section. My research was on medical demography, which is linked with the subject of public health. In addition, I wanted to study something more practical. Perhaps the people who study medicine are always ignorant, and look for something more practical. I had a chance to read the *Biennial Report* of the World Health Organisation (WHO) at Cambridge, which included the special programme on reproduction. I noticed that this programme, which used to have a very biomedical inclination, began to pay more attention to social science and even added more about women's perspectives from the 1980s onwards. Some articles were insightful, for instance on various forms of contraceptive use by women which would affect the world very differently. All of these inspired me, because I had not come across these points of view in China.
>
> (interview, Min/Zhang, K., 23/3/1999)

At Cambridge, Zhang started his PhD research, but a twist of fate changed his plans. In 1992, Zhang contributed a paper to a workshop at the Institute of Development Studies (IDS) in Brighton on research into reproductive health in rural areas of China. At this workshop he met with scholars from China and from Harvard University. From them he learned that Harvard University had applied to the Ford Foundation for a large project on reproductive health in poor rural areas. They needed Chinese scholars to participate in the research with them, and Zhang realised that this would be a chance to secure a project for his teaching and research section at Kunming:

> This was a three year research project. They asked me whether I would like to go back to China to do the research, and they explained to me how to do the project. After that I also put forward my ideas about the project. They said, 'That is enough. That is all we need to know'. I asked them, 'If I go back to China, could my teaching and research section act as an independent collaborator?'. They said, 'Yes'. Thus, I came back (to China) with the three year project.
>
> (interview, Min/Zhang, K., 23/3/1999)

After this workshop, Zhang gave up the chance of studying for the PhD at Cambridge and went back to Kunming. The first research reality that he had to face was the geographical location of Yunnan. As agricultural sector reforms in the 1980s abolished the Rural Cooperative Medical System (RCMS),[5] many of China's poorer inhabitants, who had no way of paying for medical care, suffered adverse health effects. Moreover, decreasing government involvement in public health services made access to quality health care much more difficult for poorer individuals.

Zhang Kaining also came face to face with the pronounced conservatism of the academic research milieu in Yunnan. Academically, there was no subject called 'reproductive health' in China at that time. In China, the issue of reproductive health had been handled by the field of 'maternal and child health care' (*fu you baojian*) since the 1950s. It had historically been the domain of either physicians or population planners and research on the subject had been limited to biomedicine or demographics. Medical and social scientists had traditionally worked separately in China. Likewise, government agencies had tended not to work with each other or with non-government entities. As a result,

> until 1994, neither the impact of major health reforms on reproductive health services nor that of economic and social changes had been explored thoroughly by researchers in China. There remained a lack of comprehensive, reliable information on reproductive health services and their utilisation. Past studies of health service utilisation in China typically excluded analyses of reproductive health services.
>
> (Ford Foundation, 1995: 5)

Economic reforms and subsequent social changes in China had made the recognition of the socio-cultural factors that influence women's reproductive health more urgent.

Inspired by the World Health Organisation (WHO) report, Zhang Kaining recognised that the first important task was to move beyond single discipline approaches and to understand the root causes of reproductive health problems. Thus, the first thing Zhang did when he returned to Kunming was to invite a number of social scientists and medical doctors to read the *Biennial Report* of the WHO and discuss reproductive health problems in China. This initial contact was based on a network of young intellectuals who had worked in the countryside during the Cultural Revolution. The first meeting was held at Zhang's home. A member of the YRHRA, Zheng Fan, recalled:

> I can't remember when the first meeting took place, but it was at Zhang Kaining's home. This was before the YRHRA was set up. Zhang asked me and other friends, about seven or eight people, to have a meeting at his home. We discussed several items and issues, even who would be the core members and who would be invited to join our group. I had introduced Zhao Jie (an associate professor of Gender Studies at the Yunnan Academy

of Social Science, who became Deputy Director of the YRHRA) to Zhang. I told Zhao, 'There is a connection between your work and the reproductive health of women. Would you like to join us?' So she also came to this meeting.

(interview, Min/Zheng, F., 1/10/1999)

I was curious about why the YRHRA, the first NGO to deal with reproductive health in China, was established in Kunming rather than Beijing or Shanghai, which were more 'internationalised'. When Zheng Fan came from Kunming to Manchester as a visiting scholar, I asked him about this. He responded:

Why did we organise the YRHRA in Kunming? Well, I think there are two reasons. One was that there was a common goal between us. Our generation is familiar with the countryside and the peasants.[6] We have a strong sense of responsibility to do something for them. So it was a necessity that we came together. Indeed, there were many things that needed to be done during this period. Why did we choose this project? That was because Zhang Kaining presented a paper at that workshop of the IDS (Institute of Development Studies) on reproductive health. Zhang had read the *Biennial Report* of the WHO, and he thought this was an issue that could be addressed in China.

(interview, Min/Zheng, F., 1/10/1999)

One might consider this the internal reason for setting up the YRHRA. The external reason was, I think, the impact of the UN International Conference on Population and Development (ICPC) in Cairo in 1994 and the Fourth World Conference on Women (FWCW) in 1995, as well as the growing role of foreign NGOs in China's social development. This time, the new trend of transnational feminism had arrived on the doorstep in Yunnan.

Zhang and the young scholars who met at his home formed the YRHRA in 1994.

With members from the medical, natural, and social sciences, the arts and humanities, and law, as well as activists and practitioners, YRHRA is a lively and engaged group of (mostly) young researchers. They meet once a month in Kunming, produce a newsletter, organise lectures and press briefings, translate articles into Chinese, share their work, and discuss and probe issues related to reproductive health in their province.

(Burris, 1995: 5)

This comment was made by an officer of the Ford Foundation, who had done a great deal to support the formation of the YRHRA. A community of knowledge was born in Yunnan.

The early meetings of the YRHRA mainly focused on learning, and later, workshops were conducted which combined training with creative studies. Zhang Kaining's idea was that he would share with this group all of the information he had received from abroad. The reading materials for the meetings came from the ICPC in 1994 (Zhang Kaining being one of few Chinese scholars who attended this conference), from the WHO (including documents such as the *Biennial Report* of 1992–1993), and from the International Forum for Social Sciences in Health (IFSSH). The document *Reproductive Health: A Strategy for the 1990s* (the Ford Foundation, 1991) was at the top of their reading list. The first group of workshops included the following topics:

- The women's movement, especially women's health movements in the 'Third World'.
- Quality of life: a new global focus.
- Health as a comprehensive concept and basic human right.
- Current research and challenges in family planning.
- Current research in health care and research into improving the quality of life and the quality of health care.
- Information on urgent unfulfilled needs: the prevention and control of reproductive tract infections, including sexually transmitted diseases and HIV, and the sexual and reproductive health of adolescents.
- Health for all by the year 2000.
- Reproductive health: background, rationales, and current challenges for improvement.
- Theories about poverty alleviation, gender issues, and sustainable development.

(Zhang, Zhao, Fang, and Fang, 1998: 267)

Much fresh information poured into the YRHRA in terms of travelling theory, but the group focused mainly on two hot topics: women-centred reproductive health and methods and methodology. How could these knowledges and ideas be translated into research and practice based on the local economic, cultural, and political situation? This seemed a most pressing task. The first challenge – which also gave rise to a heated debate within the YRHRA – was that of how to interpret the concept 'women-centred'.

From the ICPC in Cairo, Zhang learned that feminist scholars and activists had largely succeeded in rewriting international population policy, transforming the agenda from the achievement of demographic targets to the enhancement of women's sexual and reproductive health, choice, and rights. However, given traditional Chinese culture, what would it mean to introduce women-centred reproductive health, and why should reproductive health be women-centred? (Zhang, 1995). A series of research projects and debates were conducted around these questions at the YRHRA, and these inquiries ultimately led to the publication of the comprehensive volume *Women-Centred Reproductive Health* (Zhao, Zhang, Wen, and Yang, 1995), with contributions from 52 authors. This book included conceptual articles, definition papers, research reports, the evaluation of educational approaches, and proposals for future work. The book represented preliminary thoughts on the aforementioned issues, and although most of the authors agreed with the new call for women-centred reproductive health, they offered different interpretations of what this entailed.

What was meant by women-centred? According to Zhang Kaining:

> It seems to go without saying that reproductive health should take women as the centre. But in turning the issue carefully over in our minds, we found it necessary that it should be discussed. For example, the term 'centre' in Chinese means something like 'to get hold of' or 'to grab'. However, in English, you will usually grab hold of an 'object', and this may seem contrary to a notion of being 'women-centred'. Therefore, we needed to discuss it very carefully. Only by discussing it in detail did we fully understand what it meant and its background in the international community. More important is that, based on the Oriental culture and condition in China, how do we use it to contribute towards developing a new reproductive health service model?
>
> (Zhang, 1995: 21–22)

As an international scholar with experience of the local culture of the rural area in Yunnan, Zhang was always vigilant of the differences of the 'in-betweens' and tried to make the best use of them in his work.

For the scholars who wanted to adapt the translation of liberal feminism, the point of women's rights had to be emphasised. Zheng Fan, a sociologist, had focused on the links between women-centred and community-based and asserted that women's central role in reproductive health ought to give them certain rights and interests in present-day China. However, those rights and interests were routinely ignored in traditional communities and families. Therefore, the two major concepts involved in reproductive health – women-centred and community-based – were inextricably linked (Zheng, 1995). Zhang drew attention to reproductive health as a means to benefit women by enhancing their rights and interests in traditional communities and families. This approach reminds us that "feminism, and women's rights only make sense in terms of the imagined communities within which people live and, through their embeddedness in cultural relations and norms" (Ong, 1996: 134). Questions about how community, development, and gender could best be negotiated within existing social norms were an important concern of the YRHRA.

Zhao Jie, a deputy-director of the YRHRA, took a more radical feminist position on this issue. She pointed out:

> Because women have the main role in reproduction, reproductive health should be 'women-centred' and this is apparently deemed modern. . . . There is no fundamental difference between old and new concepts of reproductive health: both view women as a reproductive tool. Without feminist interpretation, 'women-centred reproductive health' will continue to mean 'reproductive health as the responsibility and burden of women'. Although reproductive health concerns itself with mental and social 'well-being', male-centred social-cultural values still define 'well-being'. Such values continue to discriminate against women. Women remain the tool of male-dominated society. . . . Feminism can encourage the return to maternity of the soul – of lost human rights – thereby helping women to openly express their own needs and choose the best available practices to solve their own problems. Moreover, reproductive health research based on such a new setting can contribute to the development of feminism itself.
> (Zhao, 1995: 167–168)

This is a sharp reminder of the danger that new language can easily be used to reproduce old ideas about women as nothing more than reproductive tools. As can be seen, liberal and radical feminist ideas had achieved popularity within the YRHRA.

In order to practice women-centred reproductive health in Yunnan, the YRHRA decided to support some of its members in forming a team to conduct a research project on reproductive health in rural areas. The feminist researchers in the YRHRA had to confront some key theoretical issues. One concerned the enhancement of women's sexual and reproductive health. Interestingly, rather than engaging in theoretical discussion, my interviewees in Yunnan preferred to talk about how feminist ideas on women's health were affecting their daily lives. In our conversation, Yang Guocai, a professor and member of the Bai ethnic group, told me how her opinions on women's health had changed due to her involvement in the research and activities of the YRHRA. For most Chinese people, health means absence of illness, and Yang had shared this way of thinking. According to the definition of the WHO, however, reproductive health includes women's rights over their own sexual activities and childbirth. Thus the issue of sexuality emerged from their fieldwork:

> When we went to the rural areas to do fieldwork on health education during the early 1990s, sex was a forbidden topic with both the Han people (the majority ethnic group in China) and the ethnic minority groups. Of course, sexual activity is more important than sexual discussion in their world. There

is a very rich culture of sexual activity among ethnic minority groups. If I were a writer, I could write many very interesting stories on the subject. In most ethnic minority groups, women do not see themselves as having any sexual initiative. For example, whether in an interview or a focus group, the local women never talk about their sexual activities. They told me of a local saying: 'you only see the bull scratch the wall, you never see the wall scratch the bull', and it means that women are always in a negative position in sexual activities. Of course, women have sexual desires, but in our culture we do not talk openly about them. If we apply the new concept of reproductive health, we will, hopefully, find a connection point with these traditional cultures.

(interview, Min/Yang, 24/3/1999)

What was the connection point? How was one to find this connection point? Although Yang did not go into great detail, I could feel the tension created by discussions on feminism, local culture, and the concept of reproductive health, and the effect that these discussions had had on her and other scholars in the YRHRA.

For some scholars more familiar with feminist ideas of reproductive health and asexuality, the translation (or the solution) would be more open. Fang Qing, a deputy-director of the YRHRA who had studied abroad, explicitly wanted to understand more fully the issue of women's health and described to me the feminist ideas she had gained, as well as the ways in which they had changed her outlook on women's health since she had become involved in the research and other activities of the YRHRA: "These ideas will definitely affect the way you live and the way you work". She went on to tell me the details of the sex education she had carried out as a 'case study' with her daughter. (At this time, sex education was a novel topic in China.) She then proceeded to use a gender perspective to think about education in school, women's magazines, and so on, and this led her to notice many facets of discrimination against women in Chinese society which she had never thought of before. More important, she thought, was the impact of transnational feminism on her academic development:

> In the past, you may have seen things through a very small hole, but when you discover new ideas from the outside world, such as women's studies and reproductive health, you feel that many windows have opened for you. Whatever you are doing, you are benefiting, because the philosophy behind these ideas is consistent.
>
> (interview, Min/Fang, Q., 25/3/1999)

For Fang, the sexual activity and reproductive health of women were closely linked. The problem of how to deal with the sexual – a 'forbidden' theoretical issue even today – is one that still needs to be tackled.

Feminist researchers in the YRHRA had to face the problem of how to enhance their understanding of choice and rights in their research projects focusing on reproductive health among local rural women. Some female researchers in the YRHRA, rather than being anxious about feminist research, were more concerned about how to improve the lives of local women through these projects. For example, when Zhao Jie and a group of researchers went to the village of Miao, they found:

> When we asked them (the local women) to list common local health issues in order of priority, they described many diseases to us. In the evening, they came to our rooms to tell us things that they didn't want to talk about during the daytime, for instance, about menstruation and pregnancy. But when we helped them put these health issues in order, they still put the health issues of elderly people and children at the top of the list. I discussed this problem with my colleagues. I think if you totally follow their opinions you could not put women's health issues at the top. But if you ignored their wishes, and put the women's health issues first, you might not be acting according to their needs. We really need to think through this issue. The reason why they did not put women at the top of the list is that traditional gender ideas led them to believe that as a 'normal' woman, a 'good' woman, you shouldn't think about yourself first.
>
> (interview, Min/Zhao, J., 30/3/1999)

All of this poses a dilemma which Zhao Jie and her colleagues, and probably other feminists in Third World countries, have had to deal with:

> All for the sake of the family. How can we ever hope that health policy will pay attention to women's health issues when it accepts implicitly, without question and as unchanging the very conditions which make for women's low social and health status?
>
> (Prakash, 1987, cited from Ram, 1998: 624–625)

Learning from these practical research projects, the feminist scholars and activists in the YRHRA were trying to widen the scope of discourse on women and women's bodies beyond an exclusive concern with mothering and reproduction. Following on from this, they set up a "Gender and Development Group" and started to tackle the issues of women and poverty, gender and development.

Another hot topic was the issue of methodology. It was clear from my fieldwork in the YRHRA that the affiliated researchers were very keen to learn about research methods and methodology, particularly multidisciplinary and feminist methodology. Almost every one of my interviewees discussed the issue of methodology. In Yunnan, I became aware that there was a 'methodological fever', and new terms such as PRA and VIPP (Virtualisation in Participative Programmes) were used in the development of research programmes.

In terms of method and methodology, one of the crucial aspects of the reproductive health studies was the multidisciplinary nature of research teams. In the YRHRA research and training sites in rural Yunnan, emphasis was placed on the social, economic, and cultural factors that influence reproductive health. As the scholars in YRHRA indicated:

> Specific attention is paid to bringing a social science perspective to bear on questions that have been largely the domain of the medical profession. Therefore, the case studies in these sites involve a successful dialogue and collaboration between health professionals and social scientists.
> (Zhang et al., 1998: 270)

An example from Shuangbei County may show how collaborative research into the identification of gender issues in poor rural areas is done. In Shuangbei County, a typical poor rural area in China, a UNICEF programme established a project to provide local basic medical services, but Zhang Kaining and his colleagues found that this project had spent a lot of money on acquiring medical equipment, only to realise that the equipment could not be used in the villages. One mistake, Zhang pointed out, was that the project had neglected the need for the training of local women as doctors. This was essential, because only 7 of the 127 doctors in the county were women. In order to get first-hand information, Zhang Kaining and his colleagues went to this area to investigate the problems. They travelled through mountainous regions and found that some pregnant women had to walk along the rugged trails across the mountains to see a female doctor because there was no female doctor in their village, and certainly not one who could operate the medical equipment. This revealed the fact that there was a general lack of female reproductive health personnel and that the local people needed female rural doctors urgently in this county. Based on this information, the health research team hoped that a training programme for women would be set up to meet the urgent needs of the community. Furthermore, Zhang Kaining and his research team did not follow the conventional scientific research process and simply train new female rural doctors for this community, but they attempted, instead, to apply a multidisciplinary research method to find out why there was this serious shortage of female doctors. Zhang commented:

> Subsequently, we arranged for a sociologist, Xing Wei, to look at this issue in order to get different views from other disciplines. Her investigation revealed that the problem was not only the training of female doctors. In

the past, a number of women had been trained to serve as doctors in the villages in this county, but few of them now remained. It turned out that in this county women hold an inferior social status, and this is reflected in a lack of educational opportunities. A female doctor, besides doing her own job, has to do extra work for the village. If she marries a man who lives in another village, she has to move to his village. That means she may lose her job. Not surprisingly, after training, these female doctors found it very difficult to carry on working in this environment. Since these problems cannot be sorted out by short-term measures, we took some steps to improve the ability of female doctors to handle their difficult situation. For instance, the previous training programmes were exclusively biomedical. In the new training classes, we suggested that the county government should invite older female doctors to talk about their experiences to the new female trainees in order to prepare them for the problems ahead and help them find suitable solutions. I thought that it would help these female doctors. I don't know if you would count this as an influence of women's studies or feminism on our research group (the YRHRA)?

(interview, Min/Zhang, 23/3/1999)

For Zhang, it was a key issue to include multidisciplinary methodology and social science methods, particularly a gender perspective, in the research projects. Although Zhang never said that he was a feminist, he did try very hard to absorb feminist ideas and knowledge from international documents and employ this both in research projects and in attempts to influence government policies. He noticed that the concepts of gender equality and equity were used in international documents regarding public health. On this basis, he stressed that the issue of health should be treated as an issue of rights – and by using this frame it would be obvious that Chinese women should enjoy equal rights with men (interview, Min/Zhang, 23/3/1999). He thought that these ideas should be applied in the YRHRA. As the director, Zhang was always intent on developing theoretical tools to be used in the field of reproductive health in China, and he always aimed to see these tools translated into government policies, thus allowing poor local women to benefit from these projects. In doing so, he had to develop research methods in a broad sense, beyond what is often thought of as method. This was, it might be said, a methodology for connecting the international tracks to China.

In one of Zhang Kaining's articles, "Impact of Socio-Economic Reform in Rural China on Reproductive Health Services", he addressed the problems of the financial reforms in China, which had had an enormous impact on the provision of health care services in rural areas. These reforms had increased the disparity in services received by urban inhabitants in comparison to rural inhabitants, by relatively developed areas in comparison to underdeveloped areas, and by richer households compared to poorer households. Because of the significant imbalance and inequity in reproductive health services, some vulnerable groups (not least women in poor rural areas) were at greater risk of being infected by reproductive health illness (Zhang, 2001). Through his work as a public health researcher and through his involvement with the YRHRA, Zhang had noticed that in the process of financial reform, the Chinese government had been off-loading social responsibilities onto society itself. Therefore he pointed out in the same article that government at different levels must take a more active role in reallocating resources to rebuilding and developing essential reproductive health services in the transition from a planned economy to a market economy (Zhang, 2001). Unfortunately, his observation that reform had increased the inequities in reproductive health service provisions between urban and rural inhabitants, and between rich and poor households, was heard neither by government nor by feminist scholars at the time.

There was always the danger that learning methods would become the sole aim of studying, as I found out on my last day of fieldwork in Kunming in 1999. I was invited to take part in the quarterly meeting of the Gender and Development Group of the Yunnan Academy of Social Science. An English researcher from the IDS and a representative of Oxfam were involved in organising and conducting the meeting. The new VIPP method was to be used at the meeting, and in order for this to be done 'correctly' we had to discuss and practice the procedures of VIPP. This meant that we had to write down our ideas and suggestions concerning the procedure of the meeting on slips of coloured paper, and then we had to decide upon the procedures. After two hours of practice and discussion we were still not sure if our procedure was 'appropriate' for VIPP. In the end, we ran out of time for discussion of the actual issue we had met to deal with. At this point, I had to leave the meeting to catch the train for the two-day journey back to Beijing.

I thought about this meeting during my journey back to Beijing. The event might be said to mirror the reality of women's and gender studies in China. In the name of *jiegui*, we had to connect with the international community in what was not only a very short period of time, but also in the quickest possible manner. Who knows how many times we learned only superficialities? How would we know that we had connected to the right tracks? And how many of our own tracks had been abandoned and destroyed? We still need to concern ourselves with these questions.

Follow-up stories

After my visit to Kunming in 1999, I kept in contact with my new friends in Yunnan. From 2002 to 2003, as a member of the CSWS (at that time I was a board member), I was involved in organising and working on a project entitled

"Development Project Design, Analysis, and Implementation", which was conducted by the CSWS together with the Gender and Development Group in Yunnan (YGAD) and the Shaanxi Research Institute for Women's Studies, Marriage and the Family (SRIWSMF). This gave me the opportunity to go back to Kunming in January 2003, to carry out fieldwork with members of YGAD in Yunnan.[7]

We had set up the training classes on gender and development in Xian at the end of 2002 and teamed up as a research group.[8] Because the members of our team had previously organised a number of gender training sessions for the Women's Federation of Yunnan province, we decided that we should take their training activities as our research topic and study how theories and practices related to gender and development travelled into China. Our group's research project was to be called "Knowledge Production and Reproduction: Rethinking Gender Training in the Women's Federation of Yunnan". We interviewed seven people, including key players in gender training programmes in China and cadres from the Women's Federation in Yunnan who had participated in gender training activities.

Gender training is connected with gender mainstreaming, which was promoted by the UN. It had been introduced into China with the UN Women's Conference in Beijing in 1995. NGOs first used it to educate government officials and institution leaders about gender issues; later it was disseminated through the Women's Federation and grass-roots activists (Wang and Zhang, 2010; Zhang and Hsiung, 2010; Jacka and Sargeson, 2011; Zhao, 2011).

When gender training was introduced in Yunnan in 2000, few provinces in China had any experience with gender training. Gender issues (or women's issues) had been a concern for some time in Yunnan, but attention had mainly been directed towards rural and ethnic minority women, with a focus on such topics as the feminisation of agriculture, women's reproductive health, a lack of political participation among women, the problem of female school dropouts, and the trafficking of women and children (Zhao, 2011). These kinds of gender issues had been described frequently in the context of international GAD discussions, as well as in gender training programmes during China's modernisation process.

In order to understand what gender training entailed, I attended one of the gender training classes in the Women's Cadres School of Yunnan in February 2003. The theme of this training was "Gender and Health". The aim of the classes was to increase and promote sensitivity to gender and understand the relationship between gender and issues of health in our society. The participants were the teachers and staff from the Women's Cadres School of Yunnan.

To begin with, the participants were, regrettably, unable to 'see' any gender issues at all. They either questioned whether the gender theory had come from the West or went on to inquire into the relationship between gender and equality between men and women. The training class instructors came from the All China Women's Federation of Beijing; they were very experienced and had conducted many gender training classes for a wide variety of 'trainees'. They mixed role-play with lectures on gender, and gradually the participants were convinced that there did exist differences of sex and gender in our society. The instructors proceeded to explain that sex differences are biological, while gender differences are constructed by the social environment, and that therefore, changing gender differences entails changing society.

After three days of training, I was most impressed by the point that 'the time is different, women and men are different' (an adaptation of a statement by Mao Zedong: "The time is different, the men and women remain the same"). Therefore, the Women's Federation's key mantra – 'equality between men and women' – had to be changed to 'gender equality'. A discursive change had been introduced into this training programme. I felt, however, that the change might be too soon and too great, and that we would not be able to cope with the gap between the two during this three-day training class. There was an important part missing: the history and the present situation of women/gender and health in China were not to be discussed in this class. We did not see, for instance, the history of how the maternal and child health (MCH) system – an effective socialist health system from the 1950s to the 1970s – had developed since 1949. We did not pay much attention to the severely imbalanced economic development and how this had affected access to and use of maternal and child health services, generating stark inequality between various economic strata. Without acknowledging this part of history and the importance of women/gender in relation to health, the concept of gender risked being just an empty word, disconnected from our social reality.

By the end of 2003, hundreds of cadres from the Women's Federation in Yunnan had been through gender training workshops. What they had learned from this programme was one of the questions we tackled in our research group. The participants all confirmed that gender training was very useful in that it had helped them gain some knowledge of gender and increase their professional confidence; it had also helped them to find new methods to employ in their work. Almost all of our interviewees thought that gender equality and equality between men and women were the same in context, but that gender consciousness would help them to see the problem of inequality between men and women. Furthermore, our interviewees claimed that the most important strategy was to make male leaders understand notions of gender equality, because these male leaders occupied powerful positions, and most of them were completely without awareness of gender (in)equality. If they did not change their views on gender, female cadres in the Women's Federation could do next to nothing. One interviewee said that the chair of the Women's Federation in this region planned to add the issue of gender to the curriculum at the central party school. She explained the reasoning behind this in the following manner:

> The toad may call all night, but this is nothing compared to the rooster who crows just once. This is so because the toad calls the whole night long, but as soon as the rooster crows, daylight comes. The rooster is as a key figure in our society.
>
> (interview, Qi, 23/2/2003)

Having identified the problem, the task was to start gender mainstreaming.[9] Later on, the chair of the Women's Federation in the region delivered a very stimulating lecture on the issue of gender in the party school to a large group of leading cadres from various administrative levels (interview, Qi, 23/2/2003).

Since then, the gender training programme has been further developed in party schools in Yunnan. Zhao Jie and her colleagues in the Gender and Participation Research Centre (GPRC) conducted a two-year project in which they trained the leaders and teachers of party schools in Yunnan in gender awareness and gender equality and in methods of gender analysis, helping them incorporate these subjects into the curriculum for village leaders.

For the continuance of this journey of NGOs in China, I feel that a more critical attitude toward travelling feminism should be signalled. This attitude started to emerge in the CSWS in early 2002. During a discussion by email about how to maintain the CSWS as a feminist organisation, one of its members, Zhang Naihua, noted an uneasy relationship between feminism and the field of development. Under the banner of mainstreaming gender, some development agencies have dropped the radical, transformative agenda of gender and development and have instead adopted gender as a politically correct term in order to meet the gender sensitivity requirement. Gender has become a new tool used to push a neoliberal agenda of development. The popular term 'training' within the field of development legitimises the hierarchical relationship between trainers and trainees, and the dominance of Western knowledge and experts. Money from development enterprises has also produced development professionals and caused rifts among activists (Zhang, N., email, 8/1/2012). However, Zhang's worry about the professionalisation of Chinese NGOs after the year 2000 is proving to have been warranted.

Unfortunately, neither the CSWS nor the YRHRA is active in the newly developed social space. As feminist scholars have convincingly shown, there are several 'theory brokers', including academics, international and national donors, feminist NGOs, and women's movements. These different and diverse mediators play specific roles in relation to transnational feminisms (Costa, 2014: 25), the academy and feminist NGOs being the two most important localities for the circulation, translation, and reception of feminisms. The CSWS had played the role of a theory broker in this circulation. However, as a traveller group, it suffered from the disadvantage of most of its members having permanent jobs abroad. Using holidays or working on projects enabled them to travel back to China, but this was almost the only way that they could keep in contact with their Chinese counterparts. Consequently, they lacked first-hand experience of women's and gender issues within China, mainly because it was so difficult to keep up with the speed of change within society. Without a full-time coordinator and short on first-hand experience of living in China, the traveller group was just a 'theory tour guide' for foreign researchers. At the same time, with the rapid growth of information exchange via the Internet, their Chinese counterparts could access and select information from abroad for themselves. With this uneasy relationship, the CSWS all but ceased its activities from the early 2000s.

As a local NGO, the Yunnan Reproductive Health Research Association (YRHRA) functioned as a bridge to local, national, and international organisations. However, to keep up with the trends of globalisation and professionalisation among NGOs, the YRHRA changed its name in 2007 to the Yunnan Health and Development Research Association (YHDRA) in order to "expand its scope from reproductive health to all health issues. Environment and health became a major focus with financial support from the Rockefeller Brothers Fund. YHDRA continued its multidisciplinary approach to accomplish results" (Zhang and Tung, 2009: 106). In the end, a more professional medical organisation replaced the very active and democratic NGO.

These two organisations were far from the only NGOs to have experienced severe decline. On 18 May 2014, the country's only NGO that advocated against domestic violence in particular, the Anti-domestic Violence Network (ADVN)[10] announced to the world that its 14 years of work had finally come to an end. A Chinese researcher noted that the closing down of such a large women's NGO raised serious questions:

> Is this the end of the NGO operating model where a particular state-society relationship made possible the combination of the social capital of domestic governmental bodies with the financial resources of international organizations? How can the women's movement and similar social movements develop and thrive in a new environment in a rapidly changing society? These are all extremely practical and important questions awaiting answers from the field.
>
> (Dong, 2014)

Notes

1 The CSWS published two books of translations and four books of collected papers: Wang, Zheng and Du, Fangqin (eds) (1998), *Selected Works in Gender Research*, Beijing: Sanlian Publishing House; Ma, Yuanxi; Kang, Hongjin and Du, Fangqin (eds) (2000), *Selected Translations on Gender and Development*, Beijing: Sanlian Publishing House; Centre of Women's Studies at Tianjin Normal University (ed.) (1993), *Chinese Women and Development: Status, Health and Employment*, Zhengzhou: Henan People's Press; Bao, Xiaolan (ed.) (1995), *Collection of Essays on Feminist Scholarship in the West*, Beijing: Sanlian Publishing House; Jin, Yihong and Liu, Bohong (eds) (1998), *Women and Development in China at the Threshold of the New Century: Theory, Economy, Culture, and Health*, Nanjing: Nanjing University Press; Xu, Wu; Xu, Ping; Bao, Xiaolan and Gao, Xiaoxian (eds) (2000), *Gender Analysis: Poverty and Rural Development in China*, Chengdu: Sichuan People's Press.

2 A five-year project, "Development of a Women's and Gender Studies Curriculum in China", initiated jointly by members of the CSWS and some Chinese women's studies scholars, began in 1999 with funding from the Ford Foundation. See Du (2005). I will discuss this issue in Chapter 6.

3 International organisations such as the United Nations Development Fund for Women (UNIFEM) and other UN bodies; the World Bank; regional bodies including the Asia Foundation, the Asian Development Bank, and the European Union; developed countries' embassies and development organs such as the British Department for International Development (DFID); and international non-governmental organisations (NGOs), including World Vision International (WVI), the Ford Foundation, and Oxfam. For a more detailed list, see Zhao (2011: 173).

4 However, another side of this wonderful story is that there has been a price to pay. One such price was the atrophy of the School for Women Cadres which was part of the system of the Women's Federation. I was witness to this process during my long period of research in Yunnan.

5 The RCMS was established as a three-tier system for rural healthcare access in the 1950s. The RCMS functioned on a prepayment plan that consisted of individual income contribution, a village collective welfare fund, and state subsidies. The first tier consisted of 'barefoot doctors' who were trained in basic hygiene and traditional Chinese medicine. The system of barefoot doctors was the most accessible form of healthcare, especially in rural areas. Township health centres were the second tier of the RCMS, consisting of small outpatient clinics, which primarily hired medical professionals with state subsidies. Together with barefoot doctors, township health centres were utilised for the most common illnesses. The third tier was the county hospitals, which were for the most seriously ill patients. These hospitals were primarily funded by the state, but collaborated with local systems when it came to resources (equipment, physicians, etc.).

6 Most core members of the YRHRA were schoolmates and they were sent to the countryside, where they worked and lived for several years during the Cultural Revolution.

7 The members of the Yunnan GAD group mainly came from the Yunnan Academy of Social Science, and from various universities and colleges, and were engaged in research and teaching of women's and gender studies. They petitioned international organisations and the Chinese government for sponsorship to implement development projects related to the issues of women and development in rural areas. Other members were employed by foreign NGOs and worked with gender experts and advisers involved with projects which were more focused on research, intervention, and activism.

8 The members of our team from YGAD were Zhao Jie, Tong Jiyu, Li Chunrui, Yang Jing, and me.

9 The party schools have existed for many years as part of the Chinese Communist Party system. They run educational facilities and undertake training of teachers. At almost all levels of the bureaucracy, cadres have to train in the party schools to become eligible for promotion.
10 The ADVN had 71 group members covering the country's 28 provinces, municipalities, and autonomous regions (including 37 women's federation rights protection agencies at various administrative levels, as well as 24 separate hotlines for anti-domestic violence assistance, women's shelters, legal service centres, and other grass-roots NGOs). It had more than 100 active members in the fields of law, psychology, social work, journalism, communications, and NGOs, to mention just a few. For more details about this organisation, see Dong (2014).

6 That was the past, what is the future?

After China embarked on economic reforms and began to transform its economy from a socialist planned economy to a market economy in the 1980s, the country experienced rapid economic growth and remarkable political and social changes. It is not surprising inequality increased markedly when economic growth (or gross domestic product growth) became a kind of fetish.[1] In the twenty-first century, the issue of inequality became a crucial challenge for the leadership of Hu Jintao and Wen Jiaobao, who liked to refer to China under their rule as a people-centred, harmonious society. Inequality also very much dogs the current presidency of Xi Jinping and his 'Chinese dream' of reclaiming national pride and securing personal well-being for all. In order to accomplish these goals, sustained economic growth is required along with greater equality, not least gender equality, and the infusion of sound cultural values to balance growing materialism.

It is widely acknowledged that the surging inequality in China is highly gendered. Overall, the economic reforms have had more negative consequences for women than for men, and China's successful economic development has resulted in a stark deterioration of gender equality across various socio-economic, political, and cultural domains.[2]

A recent survey on Chinese women's social status conducted by the All China Women's Federation (ACWF) and the National Bureau of Statistics of China (NBS) shows that five problems obstruct progress for Chinese women. The most serious problems are a large gap in income between Chinese men and women and the unequal allocation of economic resources. This inequality particularly limits the opportunities for rural women, who encounter grave problems such as land-grabbing and land rights infringements (News of China, 2012).

Since the turn of this century, the position of China in the world has changed dramatically. What terms such as Chinese and Western (or distinctions such as West/East and local/global) will come to mean are increasingly important questions as China continues to rise in the twenty-first century. As Chinese feminism ventures out into the world, the question of how to deal with the issue of globalisation is high on the agenda. More recently, the crisis of neoliberalism has compelled worldwide feminism to reinvent radicalism. Although feminism has not secured gender equality in China, it did offer us a vast expansion in thought and theory.

In this final chapter, I will focus on the most recent decade and review the new trends of thinking and praxis of Chinese feminism. I propose to chart not only the success stories of transnational feminisms but also the disturbing reversals due to new demands from neoliberalism and the new conservatism. I shall focus on three developments. First, the desire to *jiegui* with transnational feminism resulted in a need to rethink the homogenised dichotomies of West/East and local/global. Second, the desire to re-root feminism in local narratives of inequality produced a need to revisit another period of unfinished social revolution: the era of state socialism. Third, the desire to extend more equal citizenship rights created a new women's movement.

The desire to *jiegui* with transnational feminism resulted in a need to rethink the homogenised dichotomies of west/east and local/global

Far-reaching political and economic changes, globally as well as locally, have advanced the rethinking of *jiegui* with transnational feminism to a new stage. One trend is the emphasis on the localisation of women's and gender studies. Another is the direction that *jiegui* has been shifting to, from the West toward the rest of the world.

After the 1995 'FWCW fever' [Fourth World Conference on Women] had cooled down, a new wave of promoting women's studies in higher education swept the country. Some Chinese women's studies scholars saw the promotion of women's and gender studies as the major trend of the global feminist movement. According to these scholars, developing Chinese women's and gender studies depended on the adoption of a global perspective, regional comparisons, and local action (Du, 2001), and they secured Ford Foundation funding for a five-year project, which came to be known as "Development of Women and Gender Studies in China", which started in 2000. The project was conducted by the Centre for Women's Studies at Tianjin Normal University in collaboration with the Chinese Society for Women's Studies (CSWS). It involved more than ten women's studies centres from different universities in China and covered several disciplines. The project included doing research, writing teaching materials, and organising courses (Du, 2001). The scale of funding and resources was the largest since the 1980s.

The project provided an example of one-way travelling theory: key players in the project went to the United States to study and a group of US experts came to China to attend seminars and conferences, but most of the reading materials in the seminars were written by US feminists. That is to say, the institutionalisation of women's and gender studies, the external funding, and the one-way travelling theory are all stamped with US dominance. Tani Barlow describes this as an ideological package – a well-financed, resurgent, neoliberal, US-focused effort to establish common ground for feminism (Barlow, 2000).

Crucial questions need to be asked about this new wave of women's and gender studies in higher education. As China swiftly moves towards a market economy, how would women's and gender studies as radical thought survive the commercialisation of knowledge? As part of the productive infrastructure of the state, universities increasingly gear their activities towards supporting productivity gains, enhancing internal competitiveness, and creating an ideological climate of support for such missions. As universities continue down the path of hyper-competitiveness, the key developments seem to be professionalisation and internationalisation. The government poured large sums of money into universities at the beginning of the twenty-first century, but most of the money went to subjects concerned with technology and the market, while subjects in the social sciences and humanities received far less funding. Women's and gender studies, moreover, had to rely heavily on funding from international foundations. Paradoxically, if women's and gender studies and feminism acted as critical forces in relation to state control or the neoliberal market, its knowledge was not easily accepted by the system of higher education in China. It was thus unavoidable that there would be conflicts, negotiations, and compromises between the authorities who control universities and women's and gender studies scholars.[3]

Although the development of women's and gender studies lasted more than ten years and many women's and gender studies centres were established at universities, the discipline lacks vitality, force, and conviction in terms of knowledge production. Du Fangqin, one of the heads of the project "Development of Women and Gender Studies in China", recently admitted that the knowledge production in domestic women's studies had been somewhat disappointing, not least because the production of knowledge had failed to connect closely with 'real-world' women's and gender issues. As women's and gender studies had become increasingly institutionalised, its activities were increasingly separated from the field of gender and development existing outside the universities (Du, 2013). Moreover, the growing depoliticisation of women/gender studies in academia further accentuated the growing gap between feminist theory and feminist praxis, deepening the differences between academics and activists. Where, then, are women's and gender studies scholars and activists in the women's movement to meet?

In the same period, the terms gender, NGO (non-governmental organisation), and women organising have become part of the new discourse in the field of gender and development in the real world. The term gender, in most cases, travels along with development projects from the developed North to the developing South and from West to East. In this situation, the term gender, rather than being transmitted and received in academic circles, has been translated by the women's movement from global meaning to local practice. During my fieldwork in Yunnan, when the project of gender and development came travelling to China in the 1990s, I noticed that if you did not know how to evoke the terms gender and development, then you stood little chance of receiving funding from international development agencies. Thus, learning the new language and translating the old women's liberation theories into a new discourse of gender and development became an urgent task for women's and gender scholars and cadres in the Women's Federation. In this process, local knowledge and Marxist theory of women were neglected in the scholarship and practice of gender and development in China.

With women's and gender studies confining itself to higher education, and gender and development concentrated in the countryside, the two approaches also came to employ different research methods. Where the latter tended to undertake empirical research dealing with the problems of the real world, the former gravitated towards theoretical research focused on debates in feminist theory which came mainly from the West. Crucially, links between these two spheres of research became very sparse. The regrettable consequences were that vague and abstract notions came to replace discussions of the gender theories which ought to have been based on issues from the real world.

One of the causes of this problem was that gender and women's studies scholars have not been able to throw down the 'master's tools' (Lorde, 1984) in constructing a new field of knowledge. This, in part, is because in the mid-1990s (following the 1989 events in Tiananmen Square) the academic domain of gender and women's studies was dominated by doing projects and, thus, very much oriented towards empirical studies and external funding. As a consequence, even academics came to keep a distance from theory:

> Somehow distant from 'theory', Chinese feminism speaks first and foremost for basic social justice in a 'socialist market' situation: against poverty, abuses of women and children including child labour, economic polarisation, social disparities, corruption, money fetishism and commercialisation of cultural values; for government accountability and open policy discussion, education especially of neglected rural girls, equal employment, public medical service and women's health care, environmental protection, and so on. Its rhetoric is feminine and its concern, also in the form of social criticism, is universal.
>
> (Lin, Liu, and Jin, 1998: 115)

However, keeping a distance from theory also meant retarding the establishment of feminist scholarship in academic circles. Feminist scholars and activists were looking to NGOs for support, but most transnational NGOs wanted only experts and quantifiable results, not projects aimed at building theories, and therefore basic research was squeezed out by both government and NGOs. Dominated by doing projects, mainstream gender and women's studies had skirted basic feminist issues such as the relationship between sex and gender, gender equality and gender justice, as well as its socio-political and economic agendas. The most important aspect of this was that the interrogation of the scientific canon – one of the fundamental features of feminist scholarship – had been shelved. The discourse of mainstream academia and of international organisations, such as the UN and the World Bank, was adopted without question.

I prefer to look at this problem from the perspective of feminism as an interconnected political and academic phenomenon. In order to survive in the newly developed market economy (what might also be called state-organised capitalism), feminist research, along with all other academic endeavours, has allowed itself to be domesticated and shunted onto a more conservative track. This leaves us no choice but to look for innovative resistance to the prevailing conservative atmosphere by sharpening our theoretical tools to construct a new field of knowledge. In order to perform this task, one thing we need to do is to rework the important ideas from the imperial centres. As Raewyn Connell suggests:

> We could put this more strongly. The re-working requires a critique and transformation of the metropolitan frameworks themselves. The debates about decolonial thought, Southern theory, indigenous knowledge and postcolonial thought, though they have mostly not been gender-informed, are now vital resources for developing the sociology of gender.
> (Connell, 2014: 6)

Another question is: where, with whom, and around which topics is the future dialogue going to take place? The feminists from Eastern Europe, India, Latin America, the Middle East, and Africa, for instance, are still virtually unknown in China. In other words, feminisms from the Third World and Second World remain outside our field of vision. This global flow of feminist ideas, publications, and activism is shaped by a particular power relationship; exposing this power relationship needs to be encouraged.

Recently, things have been changing, though. The direction of *jiegui* has been shifting slightly from the West to the rest of the world. As Dai Jinhua, one of the pioneers of women's studies in China, recalled:

> We didn't realise that this narrative of China going to the world had its own ideology. When we say we move towards the world, the precondition is that we are outside of the world, so we deny the world in which we were

formerly located. In addition, when we say we move towards the world, the 'world' has been converted. At first it meant Europe and America, later merely America.

(Dai with Zou, 2014: 52)

The world we tried to ignore was the Third World which was associated with the 'non-modern backwardness' of developing countries. No one from a country steeped in the discourse of modernisation would like to link up with the 'backward' world. Thus, we have been disconnecting from the Third World in the very period in which we have sought to *jiegui* with transnational feminism.

In the post-1989 political environment, Dai Jinhua started to question the issue of China going out to the world and to reflect on the role of intellectuals in an increasingly commercialised society. The increasing gap between the rich and the poor, and the wider rural-urban divide in the 1990s, especially the severe devaluation of intellectuals, persuaded Dai to rethink her position as an intellectual in the transformation period. She has travelled around the world since the 1990s, particularly to Latin America, Asia, and Africa – the so-called Third World. These travels enabled her to witness not only the impact of capitalism on various problems, such as the confrontation between the poor and rich, but also to gain an international perspective on the global structure, post–Cold War cultural politics, and an alternative modern practice. A 'truth' with regard to political economy helped Dai to understand the power of global capital that stood (in this analysis) behind culture. Put in more direct terms: US hegemony dominated the world (see Dai with Zou, 2014).

Dai was one of the early observers of the crisis of neoliberalism, and she urged Chinese feminists to shift their vision to other parts of the world. However, the political-economic turn started a reconsideration of the relationship between state, capitalism, and feminism, and a strong demand to understand the relationship between women and capitalism emerged in feminist research circles in China. Thus, a new travelling theory – a socialist/Marxist feminism – arrived in China, but this time the theories travelled not only via the field of women's and gender studies, but also from the field of political philosophy or Marxist philosophy. The term gender justice is the key word here, and Nancy Fraser is the leading exponent.[4] A reworking of socialist feminism has begun.

The desire to re-root feminism in local narratives of equality resulted in a need to revisit the era of state socialist feminism

We know how well the ideas of *liberal* feminism travelled to China, while *socialist/Marxist* ones did not travel well at all,[5] but do we know how far this has to do with US feminism dominating the international circulation of feminist ideas, and with liberal feminism dominating other kinds of feminism in the United States?[6]

Surely, there are powers accelerating the travels of some theories and blocking the travels of others. However, one thing has been missing from the map of travelling feminisms in China, and that is socialist feminism. After the political transition following the Cultural Revolution, political, structural, and ideological support systems were replaced by a single-point agenda focused on economic growth. Women were then treated either as labourers or as an economic burden, but certainly not as a political asset. As a result, Chinese women have been looking elsewhere to find new support and new means of political participation. We witnessed how the terms gender, NGO, and women organising became part of the new discourse of women's political participation in the 1990s; gender equality and gender justice have been used frequently since the 2000s. Learning from abroad is far from over, though; Chinese women still need to learn more from and about the forgotten history of socialist women's political participation around the world.

In 2010, two conferences took place in Beijing and Shanghai, both on the themes of socialist feminism, leftist thought, and women. One of these conferences was titled "On the Differences between Socialist Women's Liberation and Western Feminism: Theory and Practice", and it was hosted by Song Shaopeng at the People's University in Beijing. The other conference was titled "Asian Left-Wing Thought and Feminisms: Retrospect and Prospect", and it was organised by Dong Limin and myself at Shanghai University. Both conferences engaged broadly with socialist feminism, one focusing in particular on the relationship between the women's liberation movement in China and Western feminisms, and the other focused on left-wing thought and feminisms. As one of the organisers of the conference at Shanghai University, I had not heard that a conference was also being planned in Beijing. That two conferences with such similar themes were planned at the same time indicates that many of us perceive socialist feminism to be the 'missing link' which may help us engage theory and practice.

In the opening remarks at the Shanghai Conference, I reviewed the history of women's studies in China and argued that Chinese women's studies had experienced two interruptions. The first interruption occurred in the 1980s, at a time when women's studies had only recently been established. This interruption came in the form of a series of intellectual 'separations', whereby women's liberation was detached from the 'socialist revolution'; the academic field of women's studies was detached from traditional knowledge production in the humanities and social sciences; and the women's movement was detached from moulding and control by the state.[7] Due to these ruptures, we had not had a chance to examine our socialist history, which ended up being discarded.

The second interruption happened in the middle of the 1990s when gender travelled to China from abroad. In order to achieve *jiegui* in the short term,

Chinese women's studies had to copy and mimic Western and transnational feminist themes, concepts, and methods. One side effect of this was that the evolution of women's studies, which had been ongoing since the 1980s, was interrupted.

Against this historical background, it is necessary to examine some difficulties faced by women's and gender studies (as well as other academic subjects) in China. The most severe problem in women's and gender studies is depoliticisation (去政治化). For some academics, part of the appeal of gender studies was that under this label they could continue to do women's studies without running the risk of being labelled feminists. For these academics, the adoption of the category of gender was a change in name, not of substance. The trend towards depoliticising academic feminism has been a striking feature of the broad changes occurring within women's studies, this problem of 'depoliticisation' being connected with the de-historicisation (去历史化) of women's and gender studies: when socialist history is no longer taught or written, depoliticisation is sure to follow.

'De-questionalisation' (去问题化) was another consequence of the institutionalisation of women's and gender studies in the late 1990s. Some scholars felt that women's and gender studies should bid farewell to the reality of women's issues and focus only on theory building. There has also followed what we might call a 'de-critique' (去批评), which points to the fact that Chinese women's studies scholars and activists have always been eager to learn about Western feminism, but often they have not questioned or challenged the dominance of Western knowledge. Although women's and gender studies scholars have noted that many of the ideas and projects, and much of the funding, came from abroad in the name of the international community, they are mostly in the dark about or are reluctant to question what role the terms gender, development, and NGO play in the neoliberal development agenda, and how this discourse has ensured that gender has attained a place within international social movements.

Consequently, many of the scholars who participated in the two conferences stated that the legacy of socialist feminism needs to be revisited.[8] Since then, "The question of how to reconsider and inherit the historical legacy of socialist feminism had already become an agenda item in a climate of 'post-revolution'" (Min and Liu, 2010: 10). However, in order to delineate the historical legacy of socialist feminism, we have to rethink and re-examine the long history of the socialist women's movement in China and in the world at large. This rethinking has already begun. As one scholar rightly notes:

> Chinese socialist feminism is marked by a strong momentum of retrospection without many prospective elements. Scholars of the group speak of socialist feminism as a 'resource', but they do not explain in what way this resource can be used for the present.
>
> (Spakowski, 2014: 16)

Noticing the problem is one thing; tackling it is, however, another. One possible line of attack was suggested by Lin Chun's rethinking of the 'social':

> This new phase of women's struggle may begin with a redefinition of the 'social' under the double pressure of post socialism and globalisation. The social realm would involve a protective and redistributive State role as well as rationally regulated market transactions but neither statist nor market dictation, which could be ensured only by socially empowered voices and forces. The embeddedness of both public power from above and participation from below defines such a realm, where women's rights are fought through community support, public deliberation, and grassroots movements, and gender norms and values are exposed, contested, and transformed.
>
> (Lin, C., 2001: 1285)

History always carries remains and debts from the past. Some Western scholars have argued that contemporary China carries very significant debts from the 'dark' period of Maoism, particularly from the Great Leap Forward (1958–1961) and the Cultural Revolution (1966–1976) (Spakowski, 2014). In addition, contemporary China also still has to face an unfinished task, originally identified by Chinese women's scholars in the 1980s,[9] namely, responding to the question of how to reconstruct the relationship between women, state, and society? How do we link the personal lives of women with the big picture of the Chinese Communist Party (CCP), the state, and society? In other words, if the old Marxist theory of women left no room for personal freedom, then how can women be articulate with personal freedoms in the theory of socialist feminism? If *nuxing* was the real subjected position of women, then what was there in theorising theory about women that would be carried out? These more complicated aspects of China's socialist past should be thought through again.

The desire for more equal citizenship rights created a new feminist movement

On 15 January 2013, Xiao Meili, a 24-year-old woman, set out on a journey from Beijing. Wearing the slogan, "Fight sexual assault, girls want freedom", she embarked on a 144-day, 2,300-km walk from Beijing to Guangzhou to raise awareness of sexual assault. Xiao is a young feminist activist, and she had been involved in various feminist activities before starting her journey. She hoped that this 'Long March' of girls could push society towards taking sexual assault on school campuses more seriously and creating a fundamental appreciation of gender equality.

Xiao Meili wasn't alone. Others were inspired by Xiao Meili's courage and followed suit in what became a campaign against domestic violence. Xiong Jing and other young feminist activists posted semi-naked pictures of themselves on the micro-blogging website Sina Weibo and the pictures circulated widely online. The women were involved in a campaign to collect 10,000 signatures for a petition against domestic violence to be sent to the Standing Committee of the National People's Congress, calling on the legislators to accelerate their work on a law proscribing domestic violence. Women again used their naked bodies as a dramatic and forceful means of making feminist issues visible to the general public and pushing legislators to speed up their action.[10]

Such radical performances and protests occur not only on the Internet but also on the streets of big cities. Some feminists claim that a new feminist movement has emerged in China (Li, S., 2014). This movement is organised by young women, most of them university students. They proclaim their civil rights and ask the government to ensure gender equality, and in so doing they set themselves apart from the older generation of the women's movement, who were more concerned about co-operation with the state and with the implementation of policies and laws. The new feminist movement is more independent and more willing to challenge and question the responsibility of the government. Using the Internet and social media, the new movement strives to use activities to disseminate feminist ideas.

One example of the new movement activism dates to 2012, when a number of universities refused to take in female applicants, even though many of them had received better scores in their entrance examinations than most male applicants. A group of girls staged an event where they shaved their heads and lined up on the street as a form of protest. In the wake of this, a group of young feminists began to investigate how widespread the practice was of refusing female students access to university, and they published their findings in a strong report. Based on this report, the campaigners sent a letter to the national Department of Education in 2013, and because news of these events had circulated widely online, the Department of Education had to issue a statement ordering universities to abolish differential treatment of male and female university applicants (Li, Y., 2014).

Today's young women face a society that has become increasingly commercialised in recent years, and the commodification of the female body is much more severe than it was 20 years ago. The exploitation of female migrant workers and students in need of jobs is much worse than previously. There is no doubt that there will be increasing numbers of young activists fighting for equal citizenship rights, but they will find it difficult to create a new feminist movement on their own. In order to fight for equal rights, they cannot solely target men and patriarchy; they must also target state-controlled capitalism and neoliberalism.

On International Women's Day in 2015, an article titled "Today, How We Discuss Equality of Men and Women", written by a young female scholar, was published in the *Paper*.[11] Where articles dedicated to Women's Day in the established newspapers concerned themselves with either the history of the women's movement or emphasised women's problems in society, this article took a different approach. This article criticised the social problems faced by young women and men and pointed out that the focus of feminist struggles should not only be the power of men but also the capitalist system (Liu X., 2015). The most interesting part of the article was the reflective way Liu talked about her own position and experience. Returning from fieldwork in a factory in Shenzhen, she had stopped for a cup of coffee in Starbucks, which she had missed a lot. Over her coffee she realised that

> as the middle class, we are living in the space of big cities, making calls on smartphones. As for female workers, who work on assembly lines 12 hours a day a thousand miles away, we are unfamiliar with their sex lives and with their feelings. In the end, I realized in the name of 'Chinese Women' how much difference there is between me and female Chinese workers. Feminist struggles in China are not just the political critique of discourse and culture; the most important thing is to support female workers in their fight for their menstruation leave and wage increases.
>
> (Liu, X., 2015)

As I read this article, I realised that young feminists are different from their forebears. Perhaps, they are developing deeper thoughts by combining book learning with involvement in social practice and time on assembly lines. How far will they go? We will have to wait and see.

The generation of feminist academics and activists who were involved in bringing new feminist notions and practices of gender equality into China in the 1980s and 1990s are about to retire from academia and NGOs. Younger feminists are going to take over the movement and wrestle with gender inequalities in their own manner. The younger feminists, however, are students of the older feminists, who have taught them and introduced feminist thought to them. The younger generation has grown up in a feminist environment within universities (Li, S., 2014). While this bodes well for women's and gender studies in higher education, I think the ultimate aim has to be much more ambitious.

Though this new women's movement is still unfolding and a sense of powerlessness surrounds their scattered activities, let us remember that a big piece is missing from this jigsaw, namely, the massive number of women workers and rural women. If this strong force is not integrated, the women's movement is but a game for a small circle of middle class women. If the 'old' NGO operating model discussed earlier has gone out of fashion in China and in the world more broadly, how can the women's movement and similar social movements develop in a rapidly changing society? These are extremely practical and important questions which await answers from the field. After a period of self-doubt and *jiegui*, Chinese feminisms are now emerging as diverse and multidimensional sites of political and cultural dialogue locally and globally.

Having here reviewed 30 years of transnational feminisms travelling into China, I hope that something in that history will help us look forward. Hopefully, this book has shed some light on our current questions and presented us with an idea of which kinds of feminisms we are going to see in the future, not only in China but also internationally.

Shortly before I finished my two-year research project in Denmark, I was invited to deliver a talk on "Transnational Feminism and Alternative Travelling Theory" at a Danish university. After the lecture, a Nordic scholar asked: "What can we learn from you (i.e., Chinese academia)?" It is perhaps time, I thought to myself, for you to answer this question by yourself.

Notes

1. For contemporary research on the issue of inequality in China, see Li, S. et al. (2013).
2. See Liu, H. (2011); Gaetano and Jacka (2013); Zang (2014); and Qi, Min, and Ærenlund Sørensen (2016).
3. See Du (2001) and Spakowski (2001).
4. A group of feminists has been mentioned in articles by contemporary Chinese scholars in these fields, Teresa L. Ebert, Nancy Hartsock, Heidi I. Hartmann, and Iris Marion Young, among them, but only Nancy Fraser's work has been translated into Chinese in substantive quantity (four volumes published by Shanghai People's Press in 2009).
5. An increasing number of papers with discussion and questions on this problem among Chinese feminists have been published lately. See Xu (2009); Song (2012); Li (2013); Min (2013); and Dai with Zou (2014).
6. Unpublished paper by Dr. Xu Feng (2014).
7. More detailed discussion on this issue appears in Chapter 2.
8. See also Song (2011, 2012); Zhu (2011); and Min (2013).
9. See Chapter 2.
10. An earlier campaign was a spin-off of the movement "Occupy Men's Toilets" in 2012.
11. The *Paper* is an online newspaper published in Shanghai. It can be found at http://www.thepaper.cn/.

References

Ahmad, Aijaz (1992) *In Theory: Classes, Nations, Literatures*, London and New York: Verso.
Alexander, M. Jacqui and Mohanty, Chandra Talpade (eds) (1997) *Feminist Genealogies, Colonial Legacies, Democratic Futures*, New York: Routledge.
Alvarez, Sonia E. (2000) "Translating the Global: Effects of Transnational Organizing on Latin American Feminist Discourses and Practices", *Meridians: A Journal of Feminisms, Race, Transnationalism*, 1 (1), pp. 29–67.
Alvarez, Sonia E.; Costa, Claudia De Lima; Feliu, Veronica; Hester, Rebecca J.; Klahn, Norma and Thayer, Millie (eds) (2014) *Translocalities/Translocalidades: Feminist Politics of Translation in the Latin/a Americas*, Durham and London: Duke University Press.
Asad, Talal (1986) "The Concept of Cultural Translation in British Social Anthropology", in James Clifford and George E. Marcus (eds) *Writing Culture: The Poetics and Politics of Ethnography*, Berkeley, Los Angeles and London: University of California Press, pp. 141–164.
Bao, Xiaolan (ed.) (1995) *Collection of Essays on Feminist Scholarship in the West*, Beijing: Sanlian (in Chinese).
Bao, Xiaolan with Xu, Wu (2001) "Feminist Collaboration between Diaspora and China", in Ping-chun Hsiung, Maria Jaschok and Cecilia Milwertz with Red Chen (eds) *Chinese Women Organising: Cadres, Feminists, Muslims, Queers*, Oxford and New York: Berg, pp. 79–100.
Barlow, E. Tani (1994) "Politics and Protocols of *Funu*: (Un) Making National Woman", in Christina K. Gilmartin, Gail Hershatter, Lisa Rofel, and Tyrene White (eds) *Engendering China, Women, Culture, and the State*, Cambridge, MA: Harvard University Press, pp. 339–359.
Barlow, E. Tani (1997) "Woman at the Close of the Maoist Era in the Polemics of Li Xiaojiang and Her Associates", in Lisa Lowe and David Lloyd (eds) *The Politics and Culture in the Shadow of Capital*, Durham and London: Duke University Press, pp. 506–43.
Barlow, E. Tani (2000) "International Feminism of the Future", *Signs, Journal of Women in Culture and Society*, 25 (4), pp. 1099–1105.
Barlow, E. Tani (2004) *The Question of Women in Chinese Feminism*, Durham: Duke University Press.
Bassnett, Susan (1991) *Translation Studies*, London and New York: Routledge.
Bassnett, Susan and Trivedi, Harish (eds) (2002) *Post-colonial Translation: Theory and Practice*, London and New York: Routledge.
Benjamin, Walter (1973) "The Task of the Translator", in Walter Benjamin (ed.) *Illuminations*, trans. Hany Zohn, London: Fontana, pp. 70–82.
Bernal, Victoria and Grewal, Inderpal (eds) (2014) *Theorizing NGOs: States, Feminisms, and Neoliberalism*, Durham: Duke University Press.
Bielsa, Esperança and Bassnett, Susan (2009) *Translation in Global News*, London and New York: Routledge.

Braidotti, Rosi (1992) "The Exile, the Nomad, and the Migrant: Reflections on International Feminism", *Women's Studies International Forum*, 15 (1), pp. 7–9.
Braidotti, Rosi (2000) "Key Terms and Issues in the Making of European Women's Studies", in Rosi Braidotti and Esther Vonk (eds) *The Making of European Women's Studies: A Work in Progress Report on Curriculum Development and Related Issues*, Netherlands: Utrecht University, pp. 12–22.
Burris, Mary Ann (1995) "Preface", in Jie Zhao, Kaining Zhang, Yiqun Wen, and Guocai Yang (eds) *Women-Centred Reproductive Health: Background, Rationale and a Multidisciplinary Discussion*, Beijing: China Social Sciences Press, pp. 4–6.
Cai, Yiping; Wang, Zheng and Du, Fangqin (eds) (1999) *Engendering the Study of History: A Documentary of the Reading Seminar on the Construction of Women's History*, Tianjin: Internal Publication (in Chinese).
Catford, John Cunnison (1967) *A Linguistic Theory of Translation*, London: Oxford University Press.
Centre of Women's Studies at Tianjin Normal University (eds) (1993) *Chinese Women and Development: Status, Health and Employment*, Zhengzhou: Henan People's Press.
Chen, Xiaoying (2007) "Ecology of NGOs in Yunnan", *21st Century Business Herald*, 9 October 2007. http://news.sohu.com/20071009/n252541670.shtml. Accessed: 12/5/2010.
Clifford, James (1989) "Notes on Theory and Travel", *Inscriptions*, 5, pp. 177–188.
Connell, Raewyn (2014) "The Sociology of Gender in Southern Perspective", *Current Sociology Monograph*, pp. 1–18. http://csi.sagepub.com/content/early/2014/03/19/0011392114524510.full.pdf+html, downloaded at Copenhagen University Library on 4/11/2014.
Costa, Claudia De Lima (2000) "Being Here and Writing There: Gender and the Politics of Translation in a Brazilian Landscape", *Signs: Journal of Women in Culture and Society*, 25 (3), pp. 727–760.
Costa, Claudia De Lima (2001) "Unthinking Gender: The Traffic in Theories in the Americas". http://lals.ucsc.edu/hemispheric_dislogues/dialogues/costa.html. Accessed: 12/5/2012.
Costa, Claudia De Lima (2014) "Introduction to Debates about Translation, Lost (and Found?) in Translation: Feminisms in Hemispheric Dialogue", in Sonia E. Alvarez, Claudia De Lima Costa, Veronica Feliu, Rebecca J. Hester, Norma Klahn and Millie Thayer (eds) *Translocalities/Translocalidades: Feminist Politics of Translation in the Latin/a Americas*, Durham and London: Duke University Press, pp. 19–36.
Dai, Jinhua (1999) *Just as in a Mirror: The Interviews of Dai Jinhua*, Beijing: Zhishi (in Chinese).
Dai, Jinhua with Zou, Zan (2014) "Cultural Mirrors and Invisible Writing: An Interview with Dai Jinhua", *China Book Review*, 4, pp. 52–62.
Davis, Kathy (2007) *The Making of* Our Bodies, Ourselves*: How Feminism Travels across Borders*, Durham and London: Duke University Press.
Davis, Kathy and Evans, Mary (eds) (2011) *Transatlantic Conversations: Feminism as Travelling Theory*, Farnham: Ashgate.
de Beauvoir, Simone (1969) *The Second Sex*, London: New English Library.
Descarries, Francine (2003) "The Hegemony of the English Language in the Academy: The Damaging Impact of the Sociocultural and Linguistic Barriers on the Development of Feminist Sociological Knowledge, Theories and Strategies", *Current Sociology*, 51 (6), pp. 625–636.
Dingwaney, Anuradha (1995) "Introduction: Translating 'Third World' Cultures", in Anuradha Dingwaney and Carol Maier (eds) *Between Languages and Cultures: Translation and Cross-Cultural Texts*, Pittsburgh and London: University of Pittsburgh Press, pp. 3–15.
Dong, Yige (2014) "The Rise and Fall of Anti-domestic Violence Network". http://chinadevelopmentbrief.cn/articles/problems-cohabitation-rise-fall-anti-domestic-violence-network. Accessed: 4/4/2015.

Du, Fangqin (1996) "International Exchange in Women's Studies of China", *Journal of Yunnan Academic Research*, 1, pp. 57–68 (in Chinese).

Du, Fangqin (1997) "My Way into Women's Studies", *Asian Journal of Women's Studies*, 3 (1), pp. 133–160.

Du, Fangqin (2001) "'Manoeuvring Fate' and 'Following the Call': Development and Prospects of Women's Studies", in Ping-chun Hsiung, Maria Jaschok, Cecilia Milwertz with Red Chen (eds) *Chinese Women Organising: Cadres, Feminists, Muslims, Queers*, Oxford and New York: Berg, pp. 237–249.

Du, Fangqin (2005) "Developing Studies at Universities in China: Research, Curriculum and Institution", *Asian Journal of Women's Studies*, 12, pp. 35–71 (in Chinese).

Du, Fangqin (2013) "From Academics to Activism: 30 Years of China's Women's Studies", *Journal of China Women's University*, 2, pp. 47–53.

Eagleton, Mary (1986) *Feminist Literary Theory: A Reader*, Oxford: Basil Blackwell.

Feng, Yuan (1996) "A Solicitation for Interpretation of the Term 'Women's Empowerment'", *Collection of Women's Studies*, 1, pp. 57–58 (in Chinese).

Ferguson, Ann (1997) "Two Women's Studies Conferences in China: Report by an American Feminist Philosopher", *Asian Journal of Women's Studies*, 3 (1), p. 161.

Ford Foundation (1991) *Reproductive Health: A Strategy for the 1990s*, New York: Ford Foundation.

Ford Foundation (1995) *Yunnan Reproductive Health Research Association (YRHRA), Kunming, Yunnan Province, China*, Beijing: Ford Foundation, Internal Publication.

Foucault, Michel (1977) *Power/Knowledge: Selected Interviews and Other Writings, 1972–1977*, New York: Pantheon Books.

Franco, Jean (1998) "Defrocking the Vatican: Feminism's Secular Project", in Sonia E. Alvarez, Evelina Dagnino and Arturo Escobar (eds) *Cultures of Politics, Politics of Cultures: Re-visioning Latin American Social Movements*, Boulder: Westview Press, pp. 278–289.

Friedan, Betty (1963) *The Feminine Mystique*, Middlesex and Maryland: Penguin Books.

Friedman, Susan Stanford (1998) *Mapping: Feminism and the Cultural Geographies of Encounter*, Princeton, NJ: Princeton University Press.

Gaetano, Arianne M. and Jacka, Tamara (2013) *On the Move: Women and Rural-to-Urban Migration in Contemporary China*, New York: Columbia University Press.

Gao, Xiaoxian; Jiang, Bo and Wang, Guohong (eds) (2002) *Gender and Development in China: A Retrospect and Future Prospect*, Xian: Shaanxi People's Publishing House (in Chinese).

Ghodsee, Kristen (2004) "Feminism-by-Design: Emerging Capitalisms, Cultural Feminism, and Women's Nongovernmental Organizations in Postsocialist Eastern Europe", *Signs, Journal of Women in Culture and Society*, 29 (3), pp. 725–753.

Gilbert, Sandra M. and Gubar, Susan (1979) *The Madwoman in the Attic: The Woman Writer and the Nineteenth-Century Literary Imagination*, New Haven: Yale University Press.

Godard, Barbara (1990) "Theorising Feminist Discourse/Translation", in Susan Bassnett and Andre Lefevere (eds) *Translation, History and Culture*, London and New York: Pinter, pp. 87–96.

Grewal, Inderpal (2005) *Transnational America, Feminisms, Diasporas, Neoliberalisms*, Durham and London: Duke University Press.

Grewal, Inderpal and Kaplan, Caren (eds) (1994) *Scattered Hegemonies: Postmodernity and Transnational Practices*, Minneapolis and London: University of Minnesota Press.

Haraway, Donna (1991) *Simians, Cyborgs, and Women: The Reinvention of Nature*, London: Free Association Books.

Harcourt, Wendy (2009) *Body Politics in Development: Critical Debates in Gender and Development*, London and New York: Zed Books.

Harcourt, Wendy (2010) "Development as if Gender Matters", *Development*, 53 (2), pp. 210–214.
Hom, Sharon (1993) "On the Translation of Special Terms of Women's Studies", in Centre of Women's Studies at Tianjin Normal University (ed.) *Chinese Women and Development: Status, Health and Employment*, Zhengzhou: Henan People's Publishing House, pp. 68–70 (in Chinese).
Hom, Sharon (1997) "Language, Culture, and (the) Intellectual's Role in Public Policy", a paper presented at "*Symposium on Feminist Philosophy and Public Policy*", Chinese Academy of Social Sciences (CASS), Institute of Philosophy, Beijing.
hooks, bell (1992) "Representations of Whiteness in the Black Imagination", in bell hooks (ed.), *Black Looks, Race and Representation*, Boston: South End Press, pp. 165–178.
Howell, Jude (1996) "The Struggle for Survival: Prospects for the Women's Federation in Post-Mao China", *World Development*, 24 (1), pp. 129–143.
Hsiung, Ping-Chun and Wong, Yuk-Lin Renita (1998) "*Jie Gui* – Connecting the Tracks: Chinese Women's Activism Surrounding the 1995 World Conference on Women in Beijing", *Gender and History*, 10 (3), pp. 470–497.
Huang, Wanling (ed.) (1995) *Reflections and Resonance*, Beijing: Ford Foundation (in Chinese).
Jacka, Tamara and Sargeson, Sally (eds) (2011) *Women, Gender and Rural Development in China*, Cheltenham and Northampton, MA: Edward Elgar.
Jackson, Stevi (1999) "Feminist Sociology and Sociological Feminism: Recovering the Social in Feminist Thought", *Sociological Research Online*, 4 (3). http://www.socresonline.org.uk/socresonline/4/3/Jackson.html. Accessed: 5/5/2004.
Jaggar, Alison M. and Young, Iris Marion (eds) (1998) *A Companion to Feminist Philosophy*, Oxford: Blackwell, pp. 108–117.
Jin, Yihong (2001) "The All Chinese Women's Federation: Challenges and Trends", in Ping-Chun Hsiung, Maria Jaschok and Cecila Milwertz with Red Chan (eds) *Chinese Women Organizing : Cadres, Feminists, Muslims, Queers*, Oxford and New York: Berg, pp. 123–140.
Jin, Yihong and Liu, Bohong (eds) (1998) *Women and Development in China at the Threshold of the New Century: Theory, Economy, Culture, and Health*, Nanjing: Nanjing University Press.
John, Mary E. (1996) *Discrepant Dislocations*, Berkeley, Los Angeles and London: University of California Press.
Judge, Joan (2008) *The Precious Raft of History: The Past, the West, and the Woman Question in China*, Stanford, CA: Stanford University Press.
Kaplan, Caren (1996) *Questions of Travel, Postmodern Discourses of Displacement*, Durham and London: Duke University Press.
Knapp, Gudrun-Axeli (2005) "Race, Class, Gender: Reclaiming Baggage in Fast Travelling Theories", *European Journal of Women's Studies*, 12 (3), pp. 249–265.
Ko, Dorothy and Wang, Zheng (2007) *Translating Feminisms in China, a Special Issue of Gender & History*, Malden, Oxford and Carlton: Blackwell.
Lefevere, André (1995) "Introduction: Comparative Literature and Translation", *Comparative Literature*, 47 (1), pp. 1–10.
Lefevere, André and Bassnett, Susan (1990) "Introduction: Proust's Grandmother and the Thousand and One Nights. The 'Cultural Turn' in Translation Studies", in Susan Bassnett and Andre Lefevere (eds) *Translation, History and Culture*, London and New York: Pinter, pp. 1–13.
Li, Huiying (1996) "Discussion on Channelling Gender Consciousness into the Mainstream of Decision-Making", *Collection of Women's Studies*, 3, pp. 5–7 (in Chinese).
Li, Huiying (1999) "The Dissemination and Study of Gender Consciousness in Mainland China", a paper presented at the conference Re-evaluation and Repositioning: Gender,

Women's Agency and Development in at the Threshold of the New Century, Boston (in Chinese).

Li, Shi; Sato, Hiroshi and Sicular, Terry (eds) (2013) *Rising Inequality in China: Challenges to a Harmonious Society*, Cambridge: Cambridge University Press.

Li, Sipan (2014) "The More Challenges to the Government Accountability from New Feminist Movement". http://www.xingbie.org. Accessed: 4/8/2014.

Li, Virginia C.; Wang, Shaoxian; Wu, Kunyi; Zhan, Wen-tao; Wong, Glenn and Burris, Mary Ann (1998) "The Women's Reproductive Health and Development Program: The Process for Planning, Development and Evaluation", in Virginia C. Li and Shaoxian Wang (eds) *Collaboration and Participation: Women's Reproductive Health of Yunnan, China*, Beijing: United Publishing House of Beijing Medical University and China Xiehe Medical University, pp. 189–227.

Li, Xiaojiang (1988) *Eve's Exploration: A Theoretical Outline of Women's Studies in China*, Zhengzhou: Henan People's Publishing House (in Chinese).

Li, Xiaojiang (1994a) "Economic Reform and the Awakening of Chinese Women's Collective Consciousness", in Christina K. Gilmartin, Gail Hershatter, Lisa Rofel, and Tyrene White (eds) *Engendering China: Women, Culture, and the State*, Cambridge, MA: Harvard University Press, pp. 360–382.

Li, Xiaojiang (1994b) "My Path to Womanhood", in Committee on Women's Studies in Asia (ed.) *Women's Studies, Women's Lives: Theory and Practice in South and Southeast Asia*, North Melbourne: Spinfex Press, pp. 100–112.

Li, Xiaojiang (1995) *Towards Women: The Report on Women's Studies in the New Era*, Zhengzhou: Henan People's Publishing House (in Chinese).

Li, Xiaojiang (1999a) "Reading *The Second Sex* at the End of the Century", *Dushu*, 12, pp. 98–103 (in Chinese).

Li, Xiaojiang (1999b) "With What Discourse Do We Reflect on Chinese Women? Thoughts on Transnational Feminism in China", trans. Zheng, Yajie, with editorial assistance by Mayfair Mei-hui Yang, in Mayfair Mei-hui Yang (ed.) *Spaces of Their Own: Women's Public Sphere in Transnational China*, Minneapolis and London: University of Minnesota Press, pp. 261–277.

Li, Xiaojiang (2000a) *Femininity? Ism: Cultural Conflict and Identity*, Nanjing: Jiangsu People's Publishing House (in Chinese).

Li, Xiaojiang (2000b) "Oscillating between the Center and Periphery – The Predicament and Breaking Out of Chinese Women's Studies", in Lin Huang and Hongqi Wang (eds) *Chinese Women's Culture*, Beijing: Wenlian Press, 1, pp. 42–54 (in Chinese).

Li, Xiaojiang (2002) "Introduction: On the Different Interpretations in Translating Gender (*xingbie*)", in Li Xiaojiang (ed.) *Culture, Education and Gender – Local Experiences and Development of Curriculum*, Nanjing: Jiangsu People's Publishing House, pp. 1–14 (in Chinese).

Li, Xiaojiang (2013) "Responding to Tani Barlow: Women's Studies in the 1980s", *Differences*, 24 (2), pp. 172–181.

Li, Xiaojiang and Zhang, Xiaodan (1994) "Creating a Space for Women: Women's Studies in China in the 1980s", *Signs*, 20 (1), pp. 137–151.

Li, Yuan (2014) "The News Report of Women's Right in 2013", *China Women's Daily*, 8/1/2014.

Liinason, Mia (2011) *Feminism and the Academy: Exploring the Politics of Institutionalization in Gender Studies in Sweden*. http://lup.lub.lu.se/luur/download?func=downloadFile&recordOId=1761928&fileOId=1776392. Accessed: 10/6/2011.

Lin, Chun (1997) "Finding a Language: Feminism and Women's Movements in Contemporary China", in Joan W. Scott, Cora Kaplan and Debra Keates (eds) *Transitions, Environments, Translations: Feminism in International Politics*, New York and London: Routledge, pp. 11–20.

Lin, Chun (2001) "Whither Feminism: A Note on China", *Signs: Journal of Women in Culture and Society*, 26 (4), pp. 1281–1286.

Lin, Chun; Liu, Bohong and Jin, Yihong (1998) "China", in Alison M. Jaggar and Iris Marion Young (eds) *A Companion to Feminist Philosophy*, Oxford: Blackwell, pp. 108–117.

Lin, Shuming (1995) *Feminist Literary Critique in China*, Guiyang: Guizhou People's Publishing House (in Chinese).

Liu, Bohong (1995) "Trends in Women's Studies in China in 1994", *Collection of Women's Studies*, 1, pp. 9–11 (in Chinese).

Liu, Bohong (1996) "When Everybody Adds the Fuel the Flames Rise High", *Collection of Women's Studies*, 1, pp. 14–19 (in Chinese).

Liu, Bohong (1999) "The Fourth World Conference on Women and Women's Studies in China", *Women's Studies, Reprinted Materials from the Press*, 2, pp. 46–51 (in Chinese).

Liu, Bohong (2001) "The All China Women's Federation and Women's NGOs", in Ping-Chun Hsiung, Maria Jaschok, Cecilia Milwertz with Red Chen (eds) *Chinese Women Organising: Cadres, Feminists, Muslims, Queers*, Oxford and New York: Berg, pp. 141–157.

Liu, Bohong and Wu, Qing (2000) "Half a Century's Retrospect and Future Prospect: Review on the 'Conference on 50 Years of Chinese Women's Theory'", *Collection of Women's Studies*, 1, pp. 44–48 (in Chinese).

Liu, Dongxiao (2006) "When Do National Movements Adopt or Reject International Agendas?: A Comparative Analysis of the Chinese and Indian Women's Movements", *American Sociological Review*, 71 (6), pp. 921–942.

Liu, Haoming (2011) "Economic Reforms and Gender Inequality in Urban China", *Economic Development and Cultural Change*, 59 (4), pp. 839–876. http://www.jstor.org/stable/10.1086/660006. Accessed: 18/3/2014.

Liu, Lydia H. (1993) "Invention and Intervention: The Female Tradition in Modern Chinese Literature", in Tani E. Barlow (ed.) *Gender Politics in Modern China: Writing & Feminism*, Durham and London: Duke University Press, pp. 33–57.

Liu, Lydia H. (1995) *Translingual Practice, Literature, National Culture, and Translated Modernity – China, 1900–1937*, Stanford, CA: Stanford University Press.

Liu, Meng; Hu, Yanhong and Liao, Minli (2009) "Traveling Theory in China: Contextualization, Compromise and Combination", *Global Networks*, 9 (4), pp. 529–554.

Liu, Xinting (2015) "Today, How We Discuss the 'Equality between Men and Women'", *Paper*, 8/3/2015. http://m.thepaper.cn/newsDetail_forward_1308473. Accessed: 8/3/2015.

Lorde, Audre (1984) *Sister Outsider: Essays and Speeches*, Berkeley, CA: Crossing Press.

Ma, Dongling and Jia, Yunzhu (2008) "Assessment Report of Gender Equality and Women's Development in Political and Decision-Making", in Tan Lin, Jiang Yongping and Jiang Xiuhua (eds) *The Green Book of Women, Report on Gender Equality and Women's Development in China (2006–2007)*, Beijing: Social Science Academic Press, pp. 424–438.

Ma, Yuanxi; Kang, Hongjin and Du, Fangqin (eds) (2000) *Selected Translations on Gender and Development*, Beijing: Sanlian (in Chinese).

McDowell, Linda (1996) "Spatialising Feminism: Geographic Perspectives", in Nancy Duncan (ed.) *Bodyspace: Destabilising Geographies of Gender and Sexuality*, London and New York: Routledge, pp. 28–44.

Meng, Yue and Dai, Jinhua (1989) *Emerging from the Horizon of History*, Zhengzhou: Henan People's Publishing House (in Chinese).

Mignolo, Walter D. (2000) *Local Histories/Global Designs: Coloniality, Subaltern Knowledges, and Border Thinking*, Princeton, NJ: Princeton University Press.

Milwertz, Cecilia (2002) *Beijing Women Organizing for Change, a New Wave of the Chinese Women's Movement*, Copenhagen: Nias Press.

Milwertz, Cecilia and Bu, Wei (2007) "Non-Governmental Organizing for Gender Equality in China – Joining a Global Emancipatory Epistemic Community", *International Journal of Human Rights*, 11 (1&2), pp. 131–149.

Min, Dongchao (1991) *The International Women's Movement, 1789–1989*, Zhengzhou: Henan People's Publishing House (in Chinese).

Min, Dongchao (1997) "From Asexuality to Gender Differences in Modern China", in Eileen J. Yeo (ed.) *Mary Wollstonecraft and 200 Years of Feminisms*, London and New York: Rivers Oram Press, pp. 193–206.

Min, Dongchao (1998) *The Continuing Process: Translation of the Words 'Feminism' and 'Gender' into Chinese*, MA dissertation submitted to the University of Manchester.

Min, Dongchao (1999) "The Development of Women's Studies: From the 1980s to the Present", in Jackie West, Minghua Zhao, Xiangqun Chang and Yuan Cheng (eds) *Women of China: Economic and Social Transformation*, Hampshire and London: Macmillan, pp. 211–224.

Min, Dongchao (2002) *Travelling Theory, Translation and the In-Between: Women's Studies in China 1980s–1990s*. PhD thesis submitted to the University of Manchester.

Min, Dongchao (2007) "Duihua (Dialogue) In-Between: A Process of Translating the Term 'Feminism' in China", in *Interventions*, 9 (2), pp. 174–193.

Min, Dongchao (2008) "'What About Other Translation Routes (East-West)?' The Concept of the Term 'Gender' Traveling into and throughout China", in Kathy E. Ferguson and Monique Mironesco (eds) *Gender and Globalization in Asia and the Pacific: Method, Practice, Theory*, Honolulu: University of Hawai'i Press, pp. 79–100.

Min, Dongchao (2013) "The Suspension of Equality: A Reflection on the Problem of Gender Equality between Men and Women since the 1990s", *Nankai Journal*, 4, pp. 26–33 (in Chinese).

Min, Dongchao and Liu Weiwei (2010) "From Equality between Men and Women to Gender Justice: Questions, Challenges and Reflections", *Collection of Women's Studies*, 5, pp. 5–11 (in Chinese).

Mohanty, Chandra Talpade (2003) *Feminism without Borders: Decolonizing Theory, Practicing Solidarity*. Durham, NC: Duke University Press.

Mohanty, Chandra Talpade (2013) "Transnational Feminist Crossings: On Neoliberalism and Radical Critique", *Signs*, 38 (4), pp. 967–991.

News of China (2012) "Five Problems Obstruct Progress for Chinese Women". http://news.china.com.cn/rollnews/2012–05/17/content_14245639.htm. Accessed: 17/05/2012.

Olson, Greta (2012) "Gender as a Travelling Concept: A Feminist Perspective", in Birgit Neumann and Ansgar Nünning (eds) *Travelling Concepts in the Humanities*, Berlin and New York: De Gruyter, pp. 205–223.

Ong, Aihwa (1996) "Strategic Sisterhood or Sisters in Solidarity? Questions of Communitarianism and Citizenship in Asia", *Indiana Journal of Global Legal Studies*, 4, pp. 107–135.

Overing, Joanna (1987) "Translation as a Creative Process: The Power of the Name", in Ladislav Holy (ed.) *Comparative Anthropology*, Oxford and New York: Basil Blackwell, pp. 70–87.

Qi, Wang; Min, Dongchao and Sørensen, Bo Ærenlund (eds) (2016) *Revisiting Gender Inequality: Perspectives from the People's Republic of China*, New York: Palgrave Macmillan.

Qi, Wenying (1997) "Improving International Women's Studies", *Collection of Women's Studies*, 3, pp. 11–13 (in Chinese).

Ram, Kalpana (1998) "Introduction: Migratory Women, Travelling Feminisms", *Women's Studies International Forum*, 21 (6), pp. 571–579.

Ribeiro, Antonio Sousa (2004) "Translation as a Metaphor for Our Times: Postcolonialism, Borders and Identities", *Portuguese Studies*, 20, pp. 186–194.

Rich, Adrienne (1987) "Notes Toward a Politics of Location", in Adrienne Rich (ed.) *Blood, Bread and Poetry*, London: Virago Press, pp. 210–231.

Robyns, Clem (1994) "Translation and Discursive Identity", *Poetics Today*, 15 (3), pp. 405–428.

Rong, Weiyi (1994) "On Simone de Beauvoir's Theory of Women's Emancipation", *Collection of Women's Studies*, 2, pp. 46–50 (in Chinese).

Rorty, Richard (1989) *Contingency, Irony, and Solidarity*, Cambridge: Cambridge University Press.

Rubin, Gayle (1975) "The Traffic in Women: Notes on the Political Economy of Sex", in Reiter Rayna R. (ed.) *Toward an Anthropology of Women*, New York: Monthly Review Press, pp. 157–210.

Said, Edward E. (1984) "Travelling Theory", in Edward Said (ed.) *The World, the Text, and the Critic*, London and Boston: Faber and Faber, pp. 226–247.

Santos, Boaventura de Sousa (1999) "Towards a Multicultural Conception of Human Rights", in Mike Featherstone and Scott Lash (eds) *Spaces of Culture, City, Nation, World*, London, Thousand Oaks and New Delhi: Sage, pp. 214–229.

Santos, Boaventura de Sousa (2006) *The Rise of the Global Left: The World Social Forum and Beyond*, London: Zed.

Scott, Joan W. (1988) *Gender and Politics of History*, New York: Columbia University Press.

Scott, Joan W. (2003) "Feminist Reverberations", *Differences*, 13 (3), pp. 1–23.

Scott, Joan W.; Kaplan, Cora and Keates, Debra (eds) (1997) *Transitions, Environments, Translations: Feminisms in International Politics*, New York: Routledge.

Simon, Sherry (1996) *Gender in Translation: Cultural Identity and the Politics of Transmission*, London and New York: Routledge.

Snell-Hornby, Mary (1990) "Linguistic Transcoding or Cultural Transfer? A Critique of Translation Theory in Germany", in Susan Bassnett and André Lefevere (eds) *Translation, History and Culture*, London and New York: Pinter, pp. 79–86.

Song, Shaopeng (2011) "Report of the Conference 'On the Differences between Socialist Women's Liberation and Western Feminism: Theory and Practice", *Journal of Shanxi Normal University (Social Science Edition)*, 7, pp. 143–149.

Song, Shaopeng (2012) "Capitalism, Socialism and Women: Why China Needs to Rebuild a Marxist Feminist Critique", *Open Times*, 12, pp. 98–112.

Spakowski, Nicola (2001) "Internationalisation of China's Women's Studies", *Berliner China Hefte*, 20 (May), pp. 79–100.

Spakowski, Nicola (2014) "Travelling Theories in Dynamic Contexts: Theory-Building in Contemporary Chinese Feminism", paper presented at special session on Travelling Theory and Cultural Translation at the 8th Annual NNC conference, A Multitude of Encounters with Asia – Gender Perspectives, Reykjavik, Iceland, 2014.

Sudo, Mizuyo (2007) "Concepts of Women's Rights in Modern China", in Dorothy Ko and Zheng Wang (eds) *Translating Feminisms in China: A Special Issue of Gender & History*, Malden, MA: Blackwell, pp. 13–34.

Swarr, Amanda Lock and Nagar, Richa (eds) (2010) *Critical Transnational Feminist Praxis*, Albany: State University of New York Press.

Tan, Shen (1992) "The Way of Localisation of Chinese Women's Studies", *Women's Studies*, pp. 11–12 (in Chinese).

Thayer, Millie (2010) *Making Transnational Feminism: Rural Women, NGO Activists, and Northern Donors in Brazil*, New York: Routledge.

Tian, He (1991) "A Dialogue with Simone de Beauvoir", *Women's Studies*, 4, pp. 7–9 (in Chinese).

Tong, Shaosu (1993) "A Speech at the Workshop on Chinese Women and Development Held at Tianjin Normal University", in Center of Women's Studies at Tianjin Normal

University (ed.) *Chinese Women and Development: Status, Health and Development*, Zhengzhou: Henan People's Publishing House, pp. 13–15 (in Chinese).

True, Jacqui (1999) "Antipodean Feminisms", in Alena Heitlinger (ed.) *Émigré Feminism: Transnational Perspectives*, Toronto, Buffalo and London: University of Toronto Press, pp. 267–294.

Tsing, Anna Lowenhaupt (1997) "Transition as Translation", in Joan W. Scott, Cora Kaplan and Debra Keates (eds) *Transitions, Environments, Translation Feminisms in International Politics*, New York and London: Routledge, pp. 253–272.

Walby, Sylvia (2002) "Feminism in a Global Era", *Economy and Society*, 31 (4), pp. 533–557.

Wan, Shanping (1988) "The Emergence of Women's Studies in China", *Women's Studies International Forum*, 11 (5), pp. 455–464.

Wang, Lingzhen (2013) "Gender and Sexual Differences in 1980s China: Introducing Li Xiaojiang", *Differences*, 24 (2), pp. 8–21.

Wang, Qi (1999) "State-Society Relations and Women's Political Participation", in Jackie West, Minghua Zhao, Xiangqun Chang and Yuan Cheng (eds) *Women of China: Economic and Social Transformation*, Hampshire and London: Macmillan, pp. 19–44.

Wang, Zheng (1993) "Three Interviews: Wang Anyi, Zhu Lin, Dai Qing", in Tani E. Barlow (ed.) *Gender Politics in Modern China*, Durham and London: Duke University Press, pp. 159–208.

Wang, Zheng (1997a) "Maoism, Feminism, and the UN Conference on Women: Women's Studies Research in Contemporary China", *Journal of Women's History*, 8 (4), pp. 126–152.

Wang, Zheng (1997b) "An Analysis of 'Female Consciousness' and 'Gender Consciousness'", *Collection of Women's Studies*, 1, pp. 14–20 (in Chinese).

Wang, Zheng and Du, Fangqin (eds) (1998) *Selected Works in Gender Research*, Beijing: Sanlian Publishing House (in Chinese).

Wang, Zheng and Zhang, Ying (2010) "Global Concepts, Local Practices: Chinese Feminism since the Fourth UN Conference on Women", *Feminist Studies*, 36 (1), pp. 40–70.

Weiler, Hans N. (2009) "Whose Knowledge Matters? Development and the Politics of Knowledge". http://web.stanford.edu/~weiler/Texts09/Weiler_Molt_09.pdf. Accessed: 12/8/2014.

Women's Studies Institute of China (ed.) (1995) *A Collection of Theses on Women's Studies in China*, Beijing: Internal Publication (in Chinese).

Woolf, Virginia (1929) *A Room of One's Own*, New York: Harcourt Brace Jovanovich.

Xie, Lihua (1995) "How Do We Face the World? – Some Thoughts on Connecting the Tracks", in Wanling Huang (ed.) *Reflections And Resonance*, Beijing: Ford Foundation, pp. 50–54 (in Chinese).

Xu, Feng (2009) "Chinese Feminisms Encounter International Feminisms", *International Feminist Journal of Politics*, 11 (2), pp. 196–215.

Xu, Feng (2014) "The Political Economy of Feminist Ideas in Transit: Production, Dissemination and Reception" (unpublished paper).

Xu, Wu (1997) "Report on the Second National Workshop on Women and Development in China, Nanjing, China, July 21 to 26, 1997" (unpublished paper).

Xu, Wu; Bao, Xiaolan; Ma, Yuanxi; Song, Yiching; Wang, Lihua; Li, Zongmin and Wu, Ga (1999) "Reflections on 'Poverty, Gender, and Development in Rural China', Chengdu, Sichuan, China, December 1–6, 1998", *Newsletter of the CSWS*, Spring, pp. 1–9.

Xu, Wu; Ma, Yuanxi and Li, Zongmin (2000) "A Series of Interrelated Educational Projects in China: Gender, Poverty, and Rural Development, March, 1998–December, 1999" (unpublished paper).

Xu, Wu; Xu, Ping; Bao, Xiaolan and Gao, Xiaoxian (eds) (2000) *Gender Analysis: Poverty and Rural Development in China*, Chengdu: Sichuan People's Press (in Chinese).

Yang, Mayfair Mei-hui (1999) "From Gender Erasure to Gender Difference: State Feminism, Consumer Sexuality, and Women's Public Sphere in China", in Mayfair Mei-hui Yang (ed.) *Spaces of Their Own: Women's Public Sphere in Transnational China*, Minneapolis and London: University of Minnesota Press, pp. 35–67.

Yiying and Yihong (1998) "Women's Theory Opens Up a New Field", *China Women's News*, 14/1/1998 (in Chinese).

Zang, Xiaowei (ed.) (2014) *Gender Discrimination and Inequalities in China*, Routledge Major Works Collection: Gender and Chinese Society, Vol. 2, London: Routledge.

Zhang, Kaining (1995) "Women-Centred Reproductive Health: Background, Rationale, and the Value of Multidisciplinary Research and Discussion", in Jie Zhao, Kaining Zhang, Yiqun Wen and Guocai Yang (eds) *Women-Centred Reproductive Health: Background, Rationale and a Multidisciplinary Discussion*, Beijing: China Social Sciences Press, pp. 3–24 (in Chinese).

Zhang, Kaining (2001) "The Impact of Social-Economic Reform in Rural China on Reproductive Health Services", paper presented at the conference on Financial Sector Reform in China, September 11–13, 2001. http://www.hks.harvard.edu/m-rcbg/Conferences/financial_sector/ImpactofSocio-economicReforminRuralChina.pdf. Accessed: 12/11/2014.

Zhang, Kaining and Tung, Jackson (2009) "Filling the Gap in Environment and Health Work in Southwest China: The Yunnan Health and Development Research Association", in *China Environment Series*, 2008/2009, pp. 106–108. http://www.isn.ethz.ch/Digital-Library/Publications/Detail/?ord538=grp1&size538=10&ots591=eb06339b-2726-928e-0216-1b3f15392dd8&lng=en&id=144075. Accessed: 12/11/2014.

Zhang, Kaining; Zhao, Jie; Fang, Qing and Fang, Tie (1998) "Multidisciplinary Participation in Reproductive Health Research and Action: The Path-Breaking Experience of YRHRA", in Virginia C. Li and Shaoxian Wang (eds) *Collaboration and Participation: Women's Reproductive Health in Yunnan, China*, Beijing: United Publishing House of Beijing Medical University and China Xiehe Medical University, pp. 267–274.

Zhang, Naihua (2001) "Searching for 'Authentic' NGOs: The NGO Discourse and Women's Organisation in China", in Ping-Chun Hsiung, Maria Jaschok, Cecilia Milwertz with Red Chen (eds) *Chinese Women Organising: Cadres, Feminists, Muslims, Queers*, Oxford and New York: Berg, pp. 159–179.

Zhang, Naihua and Hsiung, Ping-Chun (2010) "The Chinese Women's Movement in the Context of Globalization", in Amrita Basu (ed.) *Women's Movements in the Global Era: The Power of Local Feminisms*, Boulder, San Francisco and Oxford: Westview Press, pp. 157–192.

Zhang, Naihua with Xu, Wu (1995) "Discovering the Positive within the Negative: The Women's Movement in a Changing China", in Amrita Basu (ed.) *The Challenge of Local Feminisms*, Boulder, San Francisco and Oxford: Westview Press, pp. 25–57.

Zhang, Jingyuan (ed.) (1992) *Contemporary Feminist Critique*, Beijing: Beijing University Press.

Zhang, Yunmei (1991) "A Summary of Publications on Women in the Decade 1979–1989", in Xiaojiang Li and Shen Tan (eds) *Women's Studies in China*, Zhengzhou: Henan People's Publishing House, pp. 118–138 (in Chinese).

Zhao, Jie (1995) "Reconsideration of Maternity: Women's Reproductive Health, Feminism and Related Research", in Jie Zhao, Kaining Zhang, Yiqun Wen and Guocai Yang (eds) *Women-Centred Reproductive Health: Background, Rationale and a Multidisciplinary Discussion*, Beijing, China Social Sciences Press, pp. 167–181 (in Chinese).

Zhao, Jie (2011) "Developing Yunnan's Rural and Ethnic Minority Women: A Development Practitioner's Self-Reflections", in Tamara Jacka and Sally Sargeson (eds) *Women, Gender and Rural Development in China*, Cheltenham and Northampton, MA: Edward Elgar, pp. 171–189.

Zhao, Jie; Zhang, Kaining; Wen, Yiqun and Yang, Guocai (eds) (1995) *Women-Centred Reproductive Health: Background, Rationale and a Multidisciplinary Discussion*, Beijing: China Social Sciences Press (in Chinese).

Zheng, Fan (1995) "Women's Rights and Interests in Community Models of Reproductive Health", in Jie Zhao, Kaining Zhang, Yiqun Wen and Guocai Yang (eds) *Women-Centred Reproductive Health: Background, Rationale and A Multidisciplinary Discussion*, Beijing: China Social Sciences Press, pp. 205–215 (in Chinese).

Zhu, Shanjie (2011) "Summary of the Workshop on 'Asian Left-Wing Thought and Feminism': Retrospect and Future Prospect", *Journal of Shanxi Normal University (Social Science Edition)*, 4, pp. 150–154.

Index

Ahmad, Aijaz 3
All China Women's Federation (ACWF) 14, 25, 111; gender equality 116; *jiegui* (connecting with the international track) 72–6, 88–9; non-governmental organisations (NGOs) 78; theorising theory 31–3, 36–7; translation and 42–3, 45–6, 63–4, 68–9; women's studies and 18, 20, 38–9
Anti-domestic Violence Network (ADVN) 113
Asad, Talal 10
Atkinson, Ti-Grace 2
Atsushi, Shirai 21

Bao, Xiaolan 53, 95–7
Barlow, E. Tani 118
Bassnett, Susan 10, 13, 67
Basu, Amrita 79
Beauvoir, Simone de 2, 20–1, 23, 25–30
Beijing Platform for Action 73, 75, 79, 81
Benjamin, Walter 11
Bossen, Laurel 40
bourgeois feminist theory 43–4
Braidotti, Rosi 30
British Council 76
Burris, Mary Ann 92
Butler, Judith 5

capitalism 121, 126
Catford, John Cunnison 10
Chen, Muhua 74
China: civil society in 79–80, 89, 125; Cultural Revolution 17–19, 22, 28, 38; democracy and 50; domestic violence 79, 125; economic reforms 18, 32–3, 37, 71, 75, 116, 118, 120; female doctors 107–8; feminist activism 124–6; feminist history 18, 53–6; gender (*xingbie*) consciousness 74–6; gender theory 4–5, 60–5, 77; globalisation 88; humanism 19; *jiegui* (connecting with the international track) 72–3, 88; lifestyles 27; maternal and child health (MCH) system 111; May Fourth Movement of 1919 17–19, 38; modernisation 17–18, 37–8, 71–2; non-governmental organisations (NGOs) 6, 13, 89, 98; Nordic countries and 4–5; political reforms 18, 71–2, 75; public health 100, 109, 113; reproductive health 98–109; sexual assault 124; socialist feminism 121–4; socialist revolutionary movement 18; state socialism 117; transnational feminism 5; Western views 17–18
Chinese Communist Party: class struggle and 33; official discourse 68, 73, 89; women and 19, 33, 43–4, 53, 68, 73, 88–9, 124
Chinese Organising Committee 77
Chinese Society for Women's Studies (CSWS): collaborative projects 92–7, 109–10; feminist participatory principles 96; gender theory and 59, 69, 77, 82; goals of 91; minority/indigenous women 94–5; project funding 51–2, 117; translation and 8–9, 42, 51–2, 54–7, 66, 68–9; transnational feminism and 14, 92, 113
civil society 79–80, 89, 125
class inequality 71
Clifford, James 2
community-based reproductive health 103
Connell, Raewyn 120
creolisation 2
cross-cultural interpretation 9–10, 13
cultural criticism 2
Cultural Revolution 17–19, 22, 28, 38

cultural translation 10–11, 69
cultural untranslatability 10–11, 57

Dai, Jinhua 24, 47–8, 73, 120–1
Dai, Qing 26, 34
de-historicisation 123
democracy 50
Deng, Xiaoping 71
depoliticisation 123
de-questionalisation 123
development: economic 37, 71, 75; feminism and 112; gender and 38, 65, 76, 79, 81, 87, 91, 119, 123; project funding 76, 79, 91–113
dialogue *see duihua* (dialogue)
difference, theory of 19, 49, 84, 97
domestic violence 79, 125
Dong, Limin 122
Du, Fangqin 24, 27, 82–5, 92, 118
duihua (dialogue): negotiation and 41; translator of 41–2

Eagleton, Mary 21
equivalence 10
Eve's Exploration (Li) 34–5

faithful translations 11
Fang, Qing 105
female doctors 107–8
The Feminine Mystique (Friedan) 21, 23, 25–6, 29–30
feminism: capitalism and 121, 126; Chinese history of 18–31, 53–7, 88, 117; democracy and 50; gender and 64–7; influence of 26–30; knowledge production 120; liberal 121–2; local narratives of 121; second wave 25, 30, 37–8; socialist 19–20, 32, 38–9, 121–4; translation of 8–9, 88; travelling theory and 2–4, 20, 30, 36–8; U.S. hegemony 4–5, 117–18, 122–3; *see also* transnational feminism; Western feminism
feminism (term): translation of 42–3, 45–57; use in China 44–5
feminist activism 124–6
feminist dialogue: language barriers 40–1; translation and 40–1
feminist literary theory 21
Feminist Literary Theory (Eagleton) 21
feminist participatory principles 96
feminist research methods 83–4
Firestone, Shulamith 2
Ford Foundation 5, 76, 85, 94, 99, 101, 117
Foucault, Michel 3

Four Selves 32–3
Fourth World Conference on Women (FWCW) 41, 58, 72–3, 75, 77, 79–80, 85, 88, 101, 117
Franco, Jean 58
Fraser, Nancy 5, 121
Friedan, Betty 21, 23, 25–6, 29–30

Gao, Xiaoxian 32, 65, 81–3
gender (term): defining 58, 60; development and 112, 119; feminism and 64–7; interpreting 62–7; power and 64–5; sex and 66; translation of 58–67; travelling theory and 118–19; Western feminism and 57, 61–2
gender (*xingbie*) consciousness 66, 74–6
gender and development 38, 65, 76, 79, 81, 87, 91, 119, 123
Gender and Development (GAD) project 87
Gender and Development Group in Yunnan (YGAD) 110
Gender and Participation Research Centre (GPRC) 112
gender equality: difference and 28–30, 37, 111; economic reforms and 19–20, 71–2, 88; official discourse and 39, 74; socialist 18, 33, 122
gender justice 121–2
gender mainstreaming 112
gender markers 60–1
gender studies 93, 117–20, 123; *see also* women's studies
gender theory 59, 61–6, 77, 81
gender training 110–12
Gilbert, Sandra 21
globalisation: alternative thinking and 6; feminism and 88, 116–17; translation and 13; travelling theory and 4; women's studies and 80
global justice 6
Goldmann, Lucien 1
Gubar, Susan 21

Haraway, Donna 58
higher education: internationalisation of 118; professionalisation of 118; women's studies in 117–19
Hom, Sharon K. 40
Hong Kong, Western feminism and 24, 42, 46
hooks, bell 2–3, 5
Hu, Haili 49
Huang, Qizao 78

imperialism 3

Jagger, Alison 5
Jiangsu Academy of Social Sciences (JASS) 92
jiegui (connecting with the international track): transnational feminism and 117, 120–1; women's movement and 72–3, 83–5, 87–9
Jin, Yihong 9, 32

Kang, Ling 74
Kaplan, Caren 3
Knapp, Gudrun-Axeli 6
knowledge production: conditions for 8; materiality of 7; political economy of 8; power and 97

Li, Dun 84
Li, Huiying 50–1, 63–4, 73, 87
Li, Xiaojiang 23, 26, 29–30, 33–6, 38, 43–4, 46, 51, 59–60, 86
liberal feminism 121–2
Lin, Chun 9, 62, 71, 124
Lin, Shuming 21
Liu, Bohong 9, 27, 43, 63, 77, 80–1
Liu, Lydia H. 8, 60–2
localisation: travelling theory and 5; women's studies and 80, 117
Lukács, György 1

The Madwoman in the Attic (Gilbert and Gubar) 21
Marxism 29, 31
maternal and child health (MCH) system 111
May Fourth Movement of 1919 17–19, 38
Millett, Kate 2
minority/indigenous women 94–5
misreadings 1
modernisation 17–18, 37–8, 71–2
Mohanty, Chandra Talpade 7
motherhood 35

National Bureau of Statistics of China (NBS) 116
National Conference on Theoretical Research on Women 20
neoliberalism: feminism and 116–18; gender and development 6, 112, 119, 123
networking 94–5, 97
NGO Forum 77–8, 80
non-governmental organisations (NGOs): China 6, 13, 77–89; decline of 113;

project funding 80–7, 98–9, 120; transnational feminism 113; travelling feminism and 112; Yunnan Province 98–9, 101–2
Nordic countries: China and 4–5; gender theory 4–5
nuxing (female gender) 34–6

Offen, Karen 52
Olson, Greta 66
overseas Chinese scholars: marginalisation of 96; transnational feminism 76–7; *see also* Chinese Society for Women's Studies (CSWS)

participatory rural appraisal (PRA) training 94
politics of location 4
power 3, 64–5, 68–9, 97
public discourse: transnational feminism 84; women and 19–20

Qi, Wenying 21–2

radicalism 117
reproductive health 98–109
research methodology 83–4, 106–9
Rich, Adrienne 4
Rockefeller Brothers Fund 113
A Room of One's Own (Woolf) 21
Rubin, Gayle 61–2
Rural Cooperative Medical System (RCMS) 100
rural women 5, 76, 83–6, 93, 106, 116, 126

Said, Edward 1–3, 6
Santos, Boaventura de Sousa 12–13
Scott, Joan 57, 61–2
The Second Sex (Beauvoir) 2, 20–1, 23, 25–30
sexual assault 124
sexual difference 30, 34, 36, 38, 57, 59, 66, 111
sexuality 104–5
Shaanxi Research Institute for Women's Studies, Marriage and the Family (SRIWSMF) 110
Sheng, Ying 24, 45
Sichuan Women's Federation 95
socialist feminism 19–20, 32, 38–9, 121–4
socialist revolutionary movement 18
social movements 5–7
Song, Shaopeng 122
state socialism 117

Su, Hongjun 54
Sun, Xiaomei 23, 27, 45

Taiwan: feminism and 52; Western feminism and 24, 26, 42, 46
Tan, Shen 50
theorising theory 31–7, 43, 86, 119–20, 124
Third World 120–1
translation: cultural representation 9–10; cultural untranslatability 10–11, 57; *duihua* (dialogue) 41; equivalence and 10; faithful 11; of feminist works 21; globalisation and 13; intercultural 12–13; knowledge production 8; negotiation of meaning and 67; post-colonial 61; power and 68–9; shared knowledge and 12; translators and 67–8; transnational feminism and 13; unfaithful 11; visibility of the translator 11–12, 67
translation studies 9–11, 56
translator: interests of 68; revision and 12; visibility of 11–12, 67
transnational feminism: China 5, 39, 46, 75–6, 87–9; gender (*xingbie*) consciousness 75–6; globalisation and 4; *jiegui* (connecting with the international track) 72–3, 83–5, 87–9, 117, 120–1; knowledge production 7, 120; liberal feminism 51; networking 94–5, 97; non-governmental organisations (NGOs) 77–86; overseas Chinese scholars 76–7; post-colonial 85–6; radicalism 117; Second World 120; Third World 120–1; translation and 13, 41, 54–6, 66–7; travelling theory and 3–4; women's studies conferences 41, 58, 72–3, 76
travelling feminism 20, 112–13
travelling theory: alternative 6–8; approaches to 1; characteristics of 1–3; conditions for 6–7; cultural translation and 69; feminist theory and 30, 36–8, 67; imperialism and 3; localisation and 5; misreadings 1; postcolonialism and 2; power and 7; socialist/Marxist feminism 121; U.S. feminism and 117–18
travel metaphor 2–3
Trivedi, Harish 13

UNDP (United Nations Development Programme) 76
unfaithful translations 11
UNICEF 107
UNIFEM (United Nations Development Fund for Women 76

UN International Conference on Population and Development (ICPC) 101–2
United Nations 8, 75, 78, 120
United States: feminist theory 4–5, 117–18; knowledge production 8
UN World Conference on Women 73, 110

Wang, Anyi 34, 44
Wang, Zheng 52–3, 55, 61–2
Weiler, Hans N. 8
West: feminist literary theory 21; modernisation 17–18
Western feminism: development of theory 36; dominance of 69, 117–18, 122–3; information on 22–3; liberal ideas and 32, 37, 51; translations of 24, 47–8, 68–9, 72
Williams, Raymond 1
women: class inequality and 71; discrimination against 75; empowerment 96; feminism and 21, 27–8, 43–50, 53; Four Selves 32–3; gender equality 18–20, 28–30, 33, 37, 39, 71–2, 74, 88, 111, 116; gender identity 34, 37; health care 105–9; Marxist theory of 29, 31–3, 36, 38–9, 43, 46, 49, 63–5, 68–70, 74–5, 119, 124; minority/indigenous 94–5; motherhood and 35; *nuxing* (female gender) 34–6, 124; political reforms and 18–19; production and 31–2; public discourse and 19–20, 42, 106; relationship with the state 45; re-theorising of 48; rural 5, 76, 83–6, 93, 106, 116, 126; self-awareness 19, 28–31; self-improvement 32–3; sexuality 104–5; socialism and 18–20; theory about 33–4, 36, 124; Western feminism and 24–5, 48–9
women-centred reproductive health 102–6
Women's Cadres School of Yunnan 110–11
Women's Federation of Yunnan province 76, 96, 110
women's movement 47, 68
women's studies: Chinese scholars of 41–3, 45–54, 68; collaborative projects 92–7; conferences 41, 58, 72–3, 76–7, 92–7; cross-cultural interpretation 40–1, 54–6; cultural exchanges 46; establishment of 13, 18–24, 38, 122; gender (*xingbie*) consciousness 76, 122–3; gender and development 87, 119–20; gender theory 59–65, 81, 119; impact of Beauvoir on 26–30; indigenous 94–5; information on 24–5; joint activities

81–3; knowledge production 118; personal networks for 23–4; project funding 5–6, 13, 76–7, 80–7, 92–4, 117–20; promotion of 117–18; research methodology 83–4; sexual difference 34, 38; theorising theory 31–7, 43, 86, 119–20, 124; translation and 40–1, 46–54; transnational feminism 39, 81, 87–8; trends in 39; Western feminism and 24–30, 36–8, 44–5, 48–9, 51, 60, 89
women workers 126
Woolf, Virginia 21
World Bank 8, 120
World Health Organisation (WHO) 99–101
Wu, Ga 94

Xiao, Meili 124
Xie, Lihua 25
Xiong, Jing 124

Xu, Feng 36, 79
Xu, Wu 54, 56, 92, 96–7

Yang, Guocai 104–5
Yunnan Health and Development Research Association (YHDRA) 113
Yunnan Reproductive Health Research Association (YRHRA) 14, 97; development of 100–2, 113; feminist research and 98, 104–6; research methodology 102, 106–9; transnational feminism and 91; women-centred reproductive health 102–9

Zhang, Jingyuan 47–8
Zhang, Kaining 97–103, 107–9
Zhang, Naihua 56, 88, 112
Zhao, Jie 65, 86, 104, 106
Zheng, Bijun 22
Zheng, Fan 101, 103